§ *Ron Carlson Writes a Story*

Ron Carlson Writes a Story

Ron Carlson

Graywolf Press

"The Governor's Ball," from *A Kind of Flying: Selected Stories* by
Ron Carlson. Copyright © 2003, 1997, 1992, 1987 by Ron Carlson.
Used by permission of W.W. Norton & Company, Inc.

Publication of this volume is made possible in part by a grant provided by the Minnesota State Arts Board, through an appropriation
by the Minnesota State Legislature; a grant from the Wells Fargo
Foundation Minnesota; and a grant from the National Endowment
for the Arts, which believes that a great nation deserves great art.
Significant support has also been provided by the Bush Foundation;
Target; the McKnight Foundation; and other generous contributions
from foundations, corporations, and individuals. To these organiza-
tions and individuals we offer our heartfelt thanks.

Published by Graywolf Press
250 Third Avenue North, Suite 600
Minneapolis, Minnesota 55401
All rights reserved.

www.graywolfpress.org

Published in the United States of America

ISBN 978-1-55597-477-0

4 6 8 9 7 5

Library of Congress Control Number: 2007924765

Cover design: Kyle G. Hunter

Cover art: iStockphoto.com

I want to acknowledge the help and support of Carol Houck Smith,
the first reader of "The Governor's Ball," and a steady friend. Thanks
also to Bruce Jorgansen for close reading.

§   to Blair Torrey, a great teacher,
    and to all my students through the years

§
Ron Carlson Writes a Story

the big boat

THIS IS THE STORY OF A STORY. Shortly after writing "The Governor's Ball," I gave a lecture in Park City about how I thought I had written it. I didn't really think of it as a lecture at the time but as an honest tracing of my writing day, a simple narrative of the actual process of how I survived the writing of that story. In refining my notes on that talk, and in speaking to thousands of writers in classrooms and conferences, I have come to see that the way I wrote "The Governor's Ball" was not some reflexive quirk, an anomaly, but rather a clear example of the way my writing process works. It has become a process I trust.

This is a change. When I went off to teach English and writing over twenty-five years ago, I had the notion that if I covered the elements of craft with my students I could send them off into writing fiction, and that would be that. I taught with a brilliant guy who emphasized the personal heart in his class. Instead of building upward from craft, they were guided by their powerful personal visions, their dreams. Most students, of course, used both in trying to write stories about accidents and trips and sometimes the family pet. I taught craft because it was teachable. There were examples everywhere of dialogue and scene and character and imagery and point of view, etc. Vision, of course, is not teachable. Dreams are not teachable. What a person chooses to write about is not teachable. The passion a writer brings to the page is not teachable. Can writing ever be taught? The best answer to that was given obliquely by the rock musician

David Lee Roth. When asked if money could buy happiness, he said, no, but with money you could buy the big boat and go right up to where the people were happy. With a teacher you can go right up to where the writing is done; the leap is made alone with vision, subject, passion, and instinct. So a writer comes to the page with vision in her heart and craft in her hands and a sense of what a story might be in her head. How do the three come together? My thesis is the old one: they merge in the physical writing—inside the act of writing, not from the outside. The process is the teacher. Craft is part of it, and I'm going to discuss elements/approaches to craft as we go along, but there is something else.

And that is process. The process of writing a story, as opposed to writing a letter, or a research paper, or even a novel, is a process involving radical, substance-changing discovery. If you let the process of writing a research paper on *Romeo and Juliet* change the advice the Friar gives to those young people, you're headed for trouble. If you let the process of writing a story inform and change the advice an uncle gives his niece, you're probably moving closer to the truth. I've also become convinced that a writer's confidence in his/her process is as important as any accumulated craft dexterity or writing "skill."

Sometimes this can be a hard sell to beginning writers because it feels like a mystery. They see things: articles full of how-to advice or books full of finished stories accompanied by study questions. But between the nuts and bolts of prose construction, character work, dialogue strategies, and the sweep of the short masterpieces of Western literature, there may be other notes useful for the writer.

There are a lot of books about writing, and there is good

information in many of them. Years ago when I was looking for books that might be helpful, I could only find the standard anthologies, some ultrabasic primers that only went two or three steps beyond grammar, and a kind of long personal aesthetic that was many times more metaphoric than mechanical. ("Writing my book was like flying an airplane, meeting a strange woman in a labyrinth, swimming in a cold river at night"—and I'll use a lot of metaphors in this volume!) I saw all those books in the library, but I had no idea how they got there. Just their bindings seemed to make it clear that the act of writing was beyond me.

Yet I felt I had what it took. I wanted to write, and the times that I'd applied myself to it, the results had been good. But how could I get better? All those people in the library had the ticket, I felt; how could I get it? I knew grammar. I'd read the two hundred great stories of all time, eternity, the twelfth of never, and so on. So, now?

The mistake I'd made in that thinking, I see now, was confusing reading fiction and writing fiction as being similar activities. They are *related* in important ways, but *not as activities*. You have to do one in order to do the other (guess which?), and they meet in the book, that rare and beautiful object, but they are not conducted with the same posture or instruments. One is reactive and the other creative. They are as different as walking through a strange city and folding a map correctly, as timing a swim meet and swimming in a cold river at night, as flying a plane and meeting a strange woman in an airplane. A writer goes into a story with a dream/vision that is the North Star, and an understanding of craft that is the footing, and instinct/ passion that is the driving force.

these guys were
hammering on my house

THIS IS THE STORY OF a day some years ago when I was living in Salt Lake City, Utah, a lovely city really, my old home-
town. After ten years of being Mr. Carlson, an English
teacher and coach in a prep school in Connecticut, I was
doing that thing that is best phrased as "facing the void."
I had somehow written two novels that had been nicely
published by W.W. Norton, and now I had let go of the
teaching and was "trying to write." Of course, it's one thing
to knock off a couple of novels while you're holding down a
job, writing them a page a day in the forty minutes between
classes and hockey practice, and it's entirely another to be
unemployed, unoccupied, with nothing to do all the livelong
day but write. I turned to the next project, and it seemed—
since I had already written—that the way should be paved,
or smooth, or that there should at least be a way. But to me it
just looked dark. The whole day can be a hard lesson, and it
taught me some things that year that I'm still parsing. In the
morning, I took my coffee cup into the room, turned a sheet
of paper into the typewriter (some notes in this old story
will be honestly retro), and I immediately remembered that
the living room hadn't been vacuumed for eight, maybe ten
hours. So, this little book is about how I migrated from the
vacuum and all my home appliances (many of the same ones
you have) toward my writing room, that typewriter, and the
stories I had to write. There, of course, were other pressures.
There are always other pressures.

The old house demanded attention. The roof was weak, the windows were ancient, it all needed work. The poignant feature of such projects is that they involved so much money, money I didn't have. The call was to get up and become a general contractor or sit in a drafty, unpainted room and write a story.

I made plans for the things I could do, scheduling the work for after 4:00 p.m., and I hired a good handyman to commence on the rest. While he and his assistant and another guy, a big guy they'd hired from the day-labor pool at minimum wage, worked on our house, I sat in my little room with my typewriter and I typed. It was during this period that I wrote "The Governor's Ball." I wrote the draft in one day knowing that the big day laborer made more money each time he walked by my window with a plank than I would receive if I finished my story well. But even knowing that the best return might be a letter from some editor, two copies of a journal with the story in it, and a check for $34.50, I kept typing. How'd I do that? I mean these guys were hammering on my house. How'd I stay in there? That's the story I want to tell.

I've intended this little book to be a companion for beginning writers, all those people I've been meeting fifteen at a time across the country who are somewhere in their first five stories. And I mean for it to be actually helpful in its discussion of art and craft, but my main intention is just to keep you company for a few days, tell a little story, rant and rave about what I've been doing, and give you something to do after 4:00 p.m.

A day and another day and the day
before, and the library with the big boys
in the shelves, old Dreiser, old Mencken,
all the boys down there, and I went to
see them, Hya Dreiser, Hya Mencken,
Hya, hya: there's a place for me, too,
and it begins with B, in the B shelf,
Arturo Bandini, make way for Arturo
Bandini, his slot for his book, and I sat
at the table and just looked at the place
where my book would be, right there
close to Arnold Bennett; not much
that Arnold Bennett, but I'd be there
to sort of bolster up the B's, old Arturo
Bandini . . .

John Fante, *Ask the Dust*

the idea of the story idea

PEOPLE ASK A WRITER: *Where* do you get your ideas? The question has several purposes. They're not really asking *where* so that they could go out *there* and get a few, because the fact is, everyone I've ever met is already brimming with story ideas, inklings, notions, formulas, etc. They're checking to see if you (the writer) have some wacky quirks, strange interior wiring, or a secret method for locating story ideas. Also, there is often a genuine curiosity about how a writer works (how strange are you?); how did an otherwise ordinary person commence writing a story? They also sometimes want to know about a specific story they've read: Did you drop a mattress from a truck, ever play baseball, see a UFO? People ask if a story is based on your own personal experience. It's a better question than it seems because its aim is to try to determine where "real life" was so that we can measure, consider the distance to fiction. (And then think: Can I do that, cover that ground?)

But most importantly, when beginning writers ask where ideas come from they really want to know: *Are my ideas as good as your ideas?* Do they come from anywhere near the same region? Do they have the same intent? Am I even in the ballpark thinking that writing about my aunt who wouldn't get out of the bathtub, or my summer job pouring concrete, or an all-night discussion I had with my husband, or my gambling addiction, or a moment I had on the Grand Tetons when I thought I was going to fall—are any of these legitimate "ideas" that could be approached, treated, and explored in a story?

The short true answer to that question is: if it matters to you, then it is absolutely worth writing. Many times your feeling for your "idea" is as important as the so-called "quality" of the idea itself.

When people ask me the personal-experience question, my response is that I write from my personal experiences, whether I've had them or not. At first, this sounds like a joke and people laugh, but I'm not joking. Regardless of where I got the experience (or the story "idea"), I treat it personally; if it's not personal, I don't want to be involved. If it is solely intellectual, some concept or puzzle I'm tempted by (What if there were a baseball player who had killed fans with foul balls? What if Bigfoot stole my wife?), I will explore it until I find the personal element and something sparks. Having a feeling for my material means sending myself on each journey, whether I've actually been there or not, and it involves the powerful act of the imagination that good writing requires: empathy.

Writers are told to write what they know, which on the surface is good advice. It's good in that teachers started saying it to warn their students off rehashed, paper-thin science fiction (the time warp on Planet Dwindgore had us all confused) and television stories (Come on out, Rocky, we've got the place surrounded!), from which no one learned anything. They wanted their students to come closer to home, to begin to use language to grapple with challenging stories from their lives. And I'll stand with Write what you know, but I'll add: How can you know what you know until you write it? What can the process of the story teach you? Do you know everything at the moment before commencing a story? "Writing what you know" too often becomes controlling the elements of your story, and that prevents the writer from reaching beyond the facts, and those things closely related to the facts, to a place closer to the truth of her story. I want to put the advice this way: write *toward* what you know, building an inventory, and carefully using the imagination as the powerful sensing instrument it can be.

Generally, story "ideas" are garnered from three sources: a writer's own experiences, experiences the writer has heard or read about, or experiences and notions that the writer "makes up." These categories are loose, and the word "experiences" could easily be replaced with "images," or "events," "phrases," or "moments." I can think of stories of mine that came from all three areas and combinations of them. Example: I actually dropped a mattress from a truck one day; it became the germ of a story. I was there in the truck in that weather, and I saw it disappear. Example: at a dinner party years ago I listened as my friend Larry told about a summer job he once had as a tour guide in a boat that navigated an underground cavern; it became the germ for a story called "Phenomenon." I saw the cavern as he spoke, and the water and that world opened enough for me to get a hold of it. I wanted to find out more, have that experience. I wanted to go on the boat, guide my own tour. Example: I read about a foul-ball injury in a baseball game in Scottsdale, Arizona; it became the germ for "Zanduce at Second." How would a person feel, a baseball player, if he had killed people accidentally with foul balls powerfully struck into the stands? I tried to imagine myself the afternoon before a game with these lives on my conscience. Example: I saw an aircraft carrier in New

York Harbor and thought: What if the government gave these ships to single-parent families? What if my mother raised kids in such a place? That notion became the germ for "On the U.S.S. Fortitude." Sometimes (perhaps all times) you have to be tolerant of your story "ideas" and see where they want to help you go.

Why do some of our experiences and ideas become the starting points for stories and other fabulous ideas simply fail to register? I don't know. I know that people have told me about absolutely amazing experiences that have no charge for me, and other times a mundane statement will come back to me days after it was uttered and demand attention, entrance, treatment, amplification. We're consciously and unconsciously fishing all the time, trolling the world and coming up with ideas. Everyone I've ever met has story ideas. I have never met anyone who doesn't have a story idea. That's the reason I stopped telling my seatmates on planes that I was a writer. Not because of the obvious reasons, the comments on best-selling writers (which for the most part are comments on plot and taste), and not for the comments about how they were going to take a couple weeks off soon and knock off their book. But because then we'd get into the approach that I'm going after in this book; writing is exploration, it isn't neat: you can actually write a story without knowing the ending. No one wants to hear this on an airplane from some ardent type, some writer, of whom they've never heard. They want to try out their idea on me (after I promise not to steal it), and it is always an idea about casino chips that turn out to be water soluble or the history of the development of power steering or some guy (always a guy) who discovers a body, a manuscript in a box, or a surprising tattoo behind his knee.

Are these legitimate ideas for stories? Yes and no. It's a little bit like the dilemma of where to send a child to college. The truth is that it doesn't matter where she goes; it matters how she goes. If the idea matters to you, then it is worthy of exploration. That is the single criterion. If it doesn't matter to you, but you think you could sell it because you've recently (on an airplane) read a book whose central premise was not half as rich as yours, the idea is not worth writing. If you don't want to read the story, it is not worth writing. If you think it might be good enough for other people, that other people might like it, it is not worth writing. If you consider the audience of your story to be anyone other than yourself, you are inviting compromise. That is why television, with a few exceptions, is so awful. The writers there aren't in love with any of it; they can't afford to be. They work in groups and their note on what they produce is that it is good enough for the audience. They are writing for other people. I'd love to know what they read, but I'm certain I know that answer too—they don't. How could they? It would be too painful.

Years ago I was in a class with visiting writer Ed Abbey one winter quarter at the University of Utah, and among the litany of credos he announced that term was this: if you want to read a good story, you're going to have to write it yourself. You can hear his classic bravado there, but it's an honest challenge. And that feeling—*I can't wait to read this*—should carry you through the days as you write your stories.

do you have an outline?

ALL RIGHT, LET'S WRITE A STORY, or rather: let's examine the writing of the story. Not the story, the writing, not the product, the _process_. In reading we examine the story—and we are expert readers. It's what we've been trained and drilled in. To read a story is to react to it, and to write a story is to stay alert and open to the possibilities that emerge as each sentence cuts its way into the unknown. In writing we "find" the story, and our training as readers is of less help than our training as human beings, as men and women who see, feel, and intuit and who are open to possibilities.

A legitimate concern is how much do we need to know before we plunge in. The question is always posed to me this way: Do you have an outline? Do you know the ending? What percentage of the story do you know before you begin? I'll answer that specifically concerning "The Governor's Ball," and other stories, but the honest answer is: it varies. Sometimes you know the last scene, the last sentence. (Many times that great last scene ends up being the first by the time you finish.) Sometimes you know a scene that you think goes in the middle. But the minimum is simply that you must have that story "notion" (an event, an image, a phrase, a moment) and the charge of some feeling for it. That is enough. You do not need to know the whole story. In fact, it would be impossible for you to know the whole story—regardless of how many years it's been gestating in your head, how complete an outline you have for it. Even in stories where you think you have control of all the elements, there are going to be surprises and turns in the writing that you didn't anticipate. If there aren't, then the story is not going to be as solid as it should be. Simply, and others have said this: *if you get what you expect, it isn't good enough.*

Beginning a story without knowing all the terrain is not a comfortable feeling. It's uncomfortable enough in fact to keep most people away from the keyboard. In our lives we're used to knowing what we're doing, where we're going. It would be strange to get in the car and think you were going to pick up the kids at school, but not be really sure. But there are moments in the process of writing a story when you must tolerate that feeling: you stay alert to everything that is happening and by listening and watching, you find out where you are going by going there. Somebody else may get in the car.

It sounds like a mystery, and there are parts of this enterprise that remain elusive, unspeakable, but at the center what we're talking about here are the things you can learn from yourself while you are writing the story. I don't want to say more than that about finding words for our secret selves, but let's agree that we *know* more than we can fully express, and writing is a way of touching, tapping into the heart and finally locating that knowledge, ending up with more resources than we started out with.

The single largest advantage a veteran writer has over the beginner is this tolerance for not knowing. It's not style, skill, or any other dexterity. An experienced writer has been in those woods before and is willing to be lost; she knows that being lost is necessary for the discoveries to come. The seasoned writer waits, is patient, listens to her story as it talks to her. Now I've started being a little mystical here, and

I want to avoid the sense that writing is magic and not work. The story isn't going to talk to you, but things are going to happen in the heat of writing that cannot be predicted from outside the act itself. Much of a writer's work is exploration, and that involves so many things he cannot know from the outside. And we all agree that it is more comfortable to be outside the story considering it, than inside the story struggling to see it. Comfort isn't an issue.

A couple summers ago I taught at the Port Townsend Writers' Conference up on Washington's Olympic Peninsula. The conference is held at Fort Worden, a former military installation made famous because the movie *An Officer and a Gentleman* was filmed there. What is amazing about the place are the huge cement gun emplacements and underground bunkers that at one time housed sixty-ton guns and all the men necessary to guard the Strait of Juan de Fuca from foreign aggressors. These monstrous stone ruins are overgrown like Mayan temples and imbedded throughout the hilltop like some sort of vast archeological puzzle. My son Colin was nine at the time, and we tramped back and forth through these haunting structures. For a nine-year-old, it was perfect: the lost city. At one point in the dense bushes, Colin literally found an old door. We explored its chambers and many, many more. Colin led me through dark corridors and across parapets and through tunnels in the brush; he was intoxicated with happiness. At one point two small deer met us head-on as we crawled through the thicket. Later Colin took my hand as we approached another stone battlement, and he said something I will never forget. "Dad," he said, his voice rich with joy. "Don't you love it when you don't know where you're going?" I mean it sat me down right on the ancient battlements. It was a fine moment in a great day for us that summer, but he seemed to have enunciated my credo as a writer. Those moments when you are beyond your map, past your plan, without instruments, and you continue to venture further and further into the story loving not knowing where you are going.

We live in a society that doesn't offer any support or approval for ventures that aren't clearly articulated and aligned for a goal. A writer gets past this. It's going to be a mess before you're finished, and you may not have a name for the mess or understand its utilitarian purposes. There aren't words for everything. For now, we'll call it the draft of a story.

The word "idea" has always made me vaguely nervous when I'm speaking about story because it has such a neat and narrow definition. An "idea" can be articulated. And sometimes the things that impel me into a story cannot be articulated. Sometimes it is simply that I want to finish a phrase or a sentence and follow that flow. Sometimes I simply want to create an image of a mountain campsite or the lobby of a small London hotel. Are these "ideas"? Most of my "ideas" for stories would be better termed "collisions." Something strikes me, somehow gets my attention, and I remember it. I see something out of context. I hear something.

"The Governor's Ball" began with such a collision. I've selected "The Governor's Ball" because it is a story I wrote in one long day several years ago, and I remember how I wrote it, and I'm going to tour you through that story and be as frank as I can about how I survived the writing. There are other stories I could not take apart this way because I do not know as much about how I wrote them. (Writers are not obligated to explain their work, either their methods or their themes; and there's some danger in doing so. I'm an old teacher, and I'll take the risk.) My purpose here is not to gather readers in appreciation around an old story; my purpose is to take writers to the edge of each decision I made the day I typed that first draft.

I had dropped a mattress. In what we call real life I had dropped a mattress. This is an experience that had happened to me or that I—inadvertently—was the agent of. Working alone one January day I cleared out a rental house I owned in Salt Lake City, and I loaded my old Ford pickup with debris: junk, ruined wallboard, wicked carpet, and a large mattress. It was a strange cold day with low yellow clouds and a warm wind that couldn't quite thaw the old snow. On my way to the municipal landfill with this trash, I made a mistake. I took the easy route down Fifth South and onto the freeway. As soon as I got up to speed, I felt the mattress shift, and in the rearview mirror, I saw it fly from the truck bed and disappear off the elevated portion of the freeway. For a moment I was shocked.

This actually happened. Did I think of it as a story idea at the time? Only in that everything that happens is fair game. Regardless, this was the largest thing I'd ever dropped. It was doubly unusual for me, and I want to make this clear because I'm good with loading things. I've carried hundreds of loads in dozens of states in a variety of vehicles in all weathers, and I don't drop things. But there it was: gone. And apparently it had fallen a long way. I wrote a letter about the incident to my father and illustrated it with a little drawing of the mattress lifting into the air. Then it lodged in my mind quietly for a year.

What is the proper gestation period for a story, that is, between the "event" and beginning to type? Could (or should) you write a story about something that happened to you this morning? This week? This year? There are writers who can go to a dinner party and start to write the story the next morning. I have a friend who jokes that she's writing eleven days behind her life. And I like that phrase because it speaks to the advantage of "writing close"—that is, a certain immediacy, heat. I know other writers who wait and wait and wait purposely as long as they can before they begin because they know that they'll "get more" and not run out of material. The story I finished this spring was based on an event that happened to me forty years ago when I was a fry cook. The story I'm writing right now starts with an event at the Vernal, Utah rodeo sixteen years ago. There is no set measurement for the incubation period, but going in too soon can lead to a "thinner" experience. I prefer waiting "awhile," so the event/idea can stew for a while, or grow whiskers, modify, grow, change. Also, and more importantly, I wait for a while so that I know I'll be tolerant enough with the basic story idea to let it change and grow as I write. If I'm too close in time to the experience, I might be ruled, directed too much by it, not allowing all that it suggests to enter into the play of the writing.

Now what else did I know before I started "The Governor's Ball"? I thought not very much, but that isn't true. I knew Salt Lake City, which I would use as the setting. I knew the street names and I knew north from south—all you need in Utah as each town is set like a grid by the thrifty and sensible pioneers. My address in Salt Lake at the time was 1272 East 500 South. I also knew about the Governor's

Ball, where my wife and I had once been. It is a fund-raising event. In those years Scott Matheson, a fine man and one of the few Democrats in all of Utah, was governor, and they held the dinner dance at the Hotel Utah, which was an actual hotel then, a beautiful building that had served in a way as one of the crossroads of the West, before it became an office building. The ball was $200 a person or a couple, I forget, because I couldn't afford such an outing, but we had a friend who could, and he bought a table and invited us to fill two of the seats. My wife looked good in a dress, and I could dance. There is a lot of other data I knew as well, without being overtly aware of it, but we'll turn that over as we come across it. It is truthful to say that I'd lost a mattress and had been to the Governor's Ball, and about a year after both events, I started typing a story.

If a writer is any good, what he makes
will have its source in a realm much
larger than that which his conscious
mind can encompass and will always
be a greater surprise to him than it can
ever be to his reader.

Flannery O'Connor, *Mystery and Manners*

this was the first sentence

This was the first sentence:

§   I didn't know until I had the ten-ton wet carpet on top of the hideous load of junk and I was soaked with the dank rust water that the Governor's Ball was that night.

The first word of the story is I. Who's speaking? Do I know? No. Is it me? No. Should I stop and write a character sketch for this guy, a moral code, a geneaology? No. What I have done is dive in the river. For whatever reasons, I've kicked myself off the edge in regard to this story and I've started. I felt ready. That mattress had been nibbling at me for almost a year, and I didn't want it to get away. I want to read this story. So now the most important thing for me is to figure out ways not to stop. I'm going to get out of my own way every chance I get. If I need a family tree for this guy, I'll pencil it up this afternoon when I'm out of gas for the day. For now, I've put the rope in my teeth and jumped in the river. I do not know where I will come out. As a writer you can plan, you can say, I'm going to swim across this river and come out there by that blooming jacaranda. But, you're not. It is impossible from the bank to estimate the force and contour of the current of the water, let alone the temperature and the hidden obstacles. You strip off your clothes, set your glasses on a rock, take the pencil from behind your ear, bite hard on the rope, look once, and leap in. You can't think your way across.

Your journey is going to require attention and effort. The first thing we should agree on is that writing is difficult. It is a strange activity done alone in a room mostly, and it is, many times, like work. Other times it's like anything you want it to be, meeting two brothers on a train, holding tight to the tail of what seems to be a Bengal tiger, sipping Ovaltine after midnight. Other times it can be unspeakable. When you blunder onto the far shore completing the first draft, you may be far downstream, and then you can tighten the rope, walk back, place it where you want, but let's worry about that later. Now, let's swim, find out.

So how is the first sentence? It's good. It's okay for a reader, but I don't care, I can't even think that way here. It's good for the writer because it creates what I'll call inventory—there's something in it. The writer Robert Boswell says it perfectly: "'It was a dark and stormy night,' is not a terrible sentence from a reader's point of view, but it is a terrible sentence for the writer because there's no help in it. 'Lightning struck the fence post' is much better because there's that charred and smoking fence post which I might have to use later." I'm constantly looking for *things* that are going to help me find the next sentence, survive the story.

staying in the room

THE MOST IMPORTANT THING a writer can do after completing a sentence is to stay in the room. The great temptation is to leave the room to celebrate the completion of the sentence or to go out in the den where the television lies like a dormant monster and rest up for a few days for the next sentence or to go wander the seductive possiblities of the kitchen. But. It's this simple. *The writer is the person who stays in the room.* The writer wants to read what she is in the process of creating with such passion and devotion that she will not leave the room. The writer understands that to stand up from the desk is to fail, and to leave the room is so radical and thorough a failure as to not be reversible. Who is not in the room writing? Everybody. Is it difficult to stay in the room, especially when you are not sure of what you're doing, where you're going? Yes. It's impossible. Who can do it? The writer.

In my first sentence there is some inventory: the carpet, the load of junk, and the mention of the Governor's Ball. They begin to form an inventory of evidence. And with this evidence what am I trying to prove? I am trying to prove that there was a wet carpet, a load of junk, a ball. And beyond that I'll have to write to find out. I see now that those first four lines are suggestive of something I didn't know that I meant: "I didn't know until ..." I see (having completed the story) that this guy may be lying with that phrase. It's not important (useful) for me to know that when I type it. Its meaning will emerge.

I also *now* see as a reader (reactor) that I put both agendas in the first sentence: the load of junk and the ball. The former is the narrator's errand, mission, quest, throughstory, duty to himself; and the latter is his duty to his marriage, his wife, friends, society. Knowing this is absolutely of no value to the writer. None. Zero. I say that here so that we stay square with the idea that we can find out what we were up to *after it's over*, as readers. For writers, these things are (and should be) a living, impenetrable code.

Then I typed sentence number two (don't worry—I'm not going to note this story sentence by sentence):

§ It was late afternoon and I had wrestled the carpet out of our basement, with all my strength and half my anger, to use it as a cover so none of the other wet wreckage that our burst pipes had ruined would blow out of the truck onto Twenty-first South as I drove to the dump.

I was glad to let the story migrate from "real life": now it isn't a rental house, it's "our" house after a plumbing problem. Things shift (conflate, migrate) as you type a sentence and hooray for that. It's going to happen if you encourage it or not, so get out of the way. The phrase, "all my strength and half my anger," is worth noting, first for the word "anger," which is a small clue about this guy and secondly for the construction, which I will echo again in a page, though I don't know it now.

Staying in the room will permit me to catch several things (dozens in any story) that I don't even know I've thrown into the air. This is a juggling metaphor and it's apt. You write something, for example, "a blue and white wool sweater," and what you want is a real sweater, something a character would really wear, something that might help us see and believe him a little bit. What you don't know is that five pages from creating the sweater as a realistic item of your inventory, it is going to help his sister find him at the Garfield County Fair late that night. You didn't plan that, but when it happens it will seem only necessary; and staying in the room will allow it to happen.

Then I typed the third sentence of the story and completed the first paragraph:

> § The wind had come up and my shirt front was stiffening as Cody pulled up the driveway in her Saab.

Now this is simply a fabulous sentence. Think of it: a new character enters! Opportunity! A reason to go on typing! It's important to note that the sentence was typed straight out, that is, without hesitation: wind, shirt, Cody, driveway, Saab. A page of prose (and a poem even more so) represents hundreds of decisions, a causally linked series of problems to be solved. Every fourth word seems a fork (if not a cloverleaf) in the road. Who's coming? The woman. What's her name? Cody. What's her car? A Saab. Sometimes you know going in who's arriving in what. You change a person's name from Cherry to Beth, and you use her real car, an old pearl-colored Valiant with a push-button transmission. What difference does it make, though, if her name is Beth or Cherry or even Cody? If her car is an Impulse or a Skylark? Let's ask that again from the point of view of the person writing the story: What will help you stay in the room? Two things:

staying specific and not stopping. If I don't know the woman's name I simply use Doris. For a man: Mickey. I've been using Mickey and Doris in examples (and in first drafts) for twenty years. I specify all types of things; if I don't know the car, it's a Buick. I like the word Buick. To reach for your atlas, the yellow pages, your book of names, thesaurus, dictionary there at your writing desk during your writing time is a mistake. (Worse: Google, which didn't exist when I wrote this story.) You aren't looking for the right name, you're looking for a reason to stop. I personally love to cruise the yellow pages for names, though I've found atlases more helpful, *but I never do it when I'm writing.* I try to get a name I believe right away, but if it isn't right, there'll be plenty of time to set that name right after my hour or two or six at the typewriter is over. Burned-out and dizzy with success and the faint hum of carpal tunnel, I'll have all evening to locate the right name and do a ten-second search and replace.

the dictionary stand

LET'S SEARCH AND REPLACE these reference books before we get this name right. One of my closest friends is the director of a school-library system, and we'd talked about the functions of libraries for hundreds of hours. I always considered one of the fine curiosities of a library to be the dictionary stand. My friend has some beautiful oak dictionary stands in his edifice, holding their forty-pound Webster's open to the Ms and waiting for an inquiry. What I'm saying is that they struck me as quaint. First of all I don't have room in my study at home for one, and then I thought I always wanted my dictionaries close at hand, right there so I can grab it and look up *Yggdrasil* or find out just how many r's there are in *emba—assment*. I knew that the dictionary is an editor's tool, but then I learned firsthand that it is an instrument, like almost all the equipment under the roof for which you pay the rent/mortgage, which is asking you to stop writing. It sits there like the honest upright member of your library and asks you to stop typing and look something up. Don't. Instead: move that book. Get a dictionary stand and put it out by the window in the living room and lay that rich opprobrious volume on it, so you'll be reminded only later to begin to edit. That goes for Roget's work, the yellow pages, your maps, Bartlett's, Stories of the World's Great Operas, Encylopedia of Manners, Universal Recipes, the almanac, etc., etc. Get a stand for each and put them downstairs and out by the window where they'll be visible from the street and thereby raise the expectations and behavior of the general citizenry. But during your writing time, don't you touch them.

What has invaded the writer's room more than any of these editorial monitors, is the Internet, and I will just say that the Internet is the enemy of a writer's day. The Internet is a heaping helping of what everyone else is thinking—and right this minute. If you open your e-mail, you are asking to let go of the day. I don't want to belabor this obvious point, but we have welcomed this convenience right onto the very screens where we are writing stories, and e-mail is not a friend to the writer.

If you decided to paint your house and took a day and prepped it, and then with your paint ready and a roller in your hand, you decided to knock down the hornet's nest under the eave, you are going to spend the day killing hornets and being stung. Your house will not get painted, though you will have plenty of exercise. And when you go out tomorrow to paint, the hornet's nest will be there again within striking distance. The rule is that you should paint your house. Do a careful job and paint it all until you paint right up to the insects. Then you can knock at them, if you are so inclined. E-mail is a national addiction that has quietly corrupted every edge of the writer's day.

the editor's new hat

YOUR REFERENCE SOURCES are simply metaphors for the critic, teacher, reader, editor, reactor in all of us, and we must leave these people out of the room. They don't get to go in. You take off your editor's hat and check it at the door, your critic shirt, your teacher's pants, your reader's underwear, your reactionary socks, shoes, and jewelry and leave them too. The naked writer gets to enter alone and unmolested by convention and free to follow his or her native impulses as untutored and shockingly noble or base as they may be. Even if you write at a coffee shop, you must figure out a way to shed all those prudent measured selves and tap into your story in a radical way. I know a lot of people who write in coffee houses, and it has never been so convenient, since you can't go two blocks anywhere in this county without being offered an iced latte or a flagon of cappuccino, but it feels too public to me. I could take some notes or do other planning work, and I love coffee, but I would hesitate to let go and dive into my heart's work sitting somewhere in mixed company with hot beverages.

writing character: an inventory

I. naming names

Let's get back to names. I named this woman Cody, a relatively unusual name. I think I'd had a student with that name
at a high school where I'd been a visiting writer. Whenever
we name someone, we're doing some character work, some
characterization. What's the goal? A name that is believable.
A name that is apt. Nothing far out on the name continuum.
Some names are male, some are very male, some are urban,
some are rural, some educated, prissy, comic, able, careless,
and on and on. We're not looking to impart any value to the
character with the name, we're looking for credibility. I look
at the baby-name books and psychological studies about the
effects names have on people. One recent study indicated that
the most trustworthy name for a woman, a woman you'd want
as your doctor and treasurer, is Beth. That doesn't mean that
the Beth in our story can't worship the Devil and print coun-
terfeit store coupons, in fact it opens that door. If you name
a character Orville, you're going to have to earn him back a
little. That is, except for secondary characters, you shouldn't
let the name do even 30 percent of the work. If Orville turns
out to be those things that we expect Orville to be, some guy
in overalls, then perhaps he should be the lawyer in the piece.
Actually Orville is an interesting name, isn't it? He and Wilbur
were force-ten bright and force-ten brave. But those names
seem dated and quaint to us.

Okay, there's nothing here you don't already know. Get

a good specific name, and stay with it. Do we base characters on people we know? Yes. Could we use their names? No.
Never. We don't keep a real name because ultimately it isn't
going to be an instrument that will help us write the story.
There's some energy at first, of course, from trading on the
real name, real character, but it fades. Example: a writer has
been through a divorce. She starts writing a story wherein a
character named Sterling, which in fact is the name of her
former husband, makes a vivid fool out of himself in arguing
about their old bentwood rocker. Well, she based the scene
on a real moment she had with her real husband Sterling,
and just typing the way his face changes as he screams about
her inability to care for the chair properly gives the writer
a big charge. She's grinning and having fun—for now. But
will this Sterling have the opportunity to surprise her later
by dropping off the bottle of wood-nourishing oil, or do
anything that the other Sterling didn't do? There is going to
come a moment when we are no longer reporting the moment, but when fiction requires that we go beyond a bad
scene in a tough time involving a nice old chair and reach
for the story. I want to advise that writer to change Sterling
to Mickey and to use the same emotional charge she has for
the scene to power her through it by listening to every little
detail. What truth of the scene is trying to emerge? That
Mickey is a rattling avaricious dolt? Perhaps, but isn't there
even something more that this ugly scene can reveal?

You are the writer; you have the power, and you've got
to be careful with it. You want to hurt people with the force
of your poignant story, not because you used their name in
a situation they're going to recognize anyway. Besides, and
this is important: you're not chained to the person. You may

begin to base a character on your college roommate (everybody else does), but you change his name from Roger to Eldon because this character is going to evolve. You need him to be free to be true to the vicissitudes of your story and not be locked into the events that actually transpired.

My wife and I taught for ten years at a prep school in Connecticut, where we encountered a certain genre of name. Every June, I would send my dear friend David Kranes in Utah the Hotchkiss graduation program, and he'd send me the program from the Salt Palace Rodeo. I still have a file of names, among other things, and I consult it sometimes— *after* my writing time to see what might be available.

2. personal inventory: detailing the status life

Then, of course, I gave Cody a Saab. Are you doing character work when you give someone a car? Yes. What's the goal? Credibility. All I want to do is believe it without being generic. What I don't see (and again I don't need to be aware of everything that's operating as I type) is that I've created two extremes: her nice imported car and his old truck. What does that mean? I don't know; if they're believable vehicles (data/inventory), then they will be their own meaning.

Do cars have various values? Yes. Should the nun drive a Jeep? Should the pimp drive a Cadillac? He can, of course. But I'm going to name my pimp Orville and put him in a Yugo.

This notion of inventory is an important consideration in creating character. Everything you give a character is another element in his or her definition and will help determine the weight s/he gives or receives in the story. If we start right at the body and radiate outward, we see hundreds of believable opportunities to give our characters unique inventories.

The Body. The body is a charmed and potent field that has been well traveled by the jillion writers before us, and it is their footsteps that have created so many wicked clichés into which the novice often stumbles. This thing first: you are not obligated to give the body. Genre writers (thriller/romance/adventure) are obligated to give the body, and you can look it up. On page 24 of every bodice-ripper there is the "tall dark and something" paragraph that goes something like: "Jim came striding out of the bunkhouse, the most beautiful man Janey had ever seen in jeans. His muscular stomach and the cords in his neck and the white flecks of starlight in his steely gray eyes thrilled her to the depths of her . . ."

We, however, are not required to meet that convention—a good fiction writer is creating her own conventions. The body may be important to your story, and you may want to shine a light on a facet of it so that the reader can better imagine and thereby follow the character, but don't stop the story to do it. The attributes you give the body should play a part in the story and not feel like furniture we need to lug along. It sounds as if I'm saying that if you give Jim a rippling washboard stomach on page 2 then he should use it to clean some clothes on page 10; what we want is to have physical details that are simply believable at first and convincingly brought forward or visited again.

Scars, tattoos, jewelry, body jewelry, hair, dental aberrations, deformities, missing digits, horns protruding through the scalp, etc. These close things are powerful: be careful. Tattoos, which took so much of their meaning from sailors and convicts, are losing some of their potency as character signals because so many of our students have decided to so adorn themselves. I saw a beautiful tattoo recently on a young man at the University of Alaska: a steaming cup of coffee on the back of his shoulder; and as I write this I have a fine young student who has more skulls on his forearm than a country graveyard. So we're warned: we don't give the concert pianist long, slender delicate fingers; we don't give the convict a three-day beard and a sneer. We don't give anyone, except perhaps the comely princess who is our very heroine, a sneer.

On the body—part is better than whole. Don't be encyclopedic from head to toe. Use the cowlick or the brown tooth or one single thing that we can believe and hold onto.

Then of course our inventory moves to clothing, the choices, such as a sharkskin suit that I'd like to see one of again, or a guy in nothing but clothing from a tony catalogue, say J. Crew, or a girl in a Grateful Dead T-shirt cut off at the midriff, etc. Everything is inventory; everything is evidence. We want to create something real enough to believe in.

The room: the dorm room, office, car interior, or whatever space is your character's space. What is on her car seat as you slide into her Pontiac? What is on his refrigerator? What is on the credenza behind his desk? What is a credenza?

To think about selecting inventory, consider this:

Mickey and Doris work at the same insurance firm as claims adjusters. After Mickey's divorce, Doris invites him out to dinner. Afterward they go to her apartment for a drink. Write the paragraph where they enter the apartment. Include three things which he sees. Then this: the following Saturday he invites her over to his place to watch the Notre Dame game. Write the paragraph where he attends to three things in his apartment before she arrives.

Our rule for now shall be: include things. Not because we're trying to clutter our stories up so that the sheer catalogues of clothing, furniture, drinks, sporting equipment make their own kind of effluvial music, or because we want to select the most symbolic or meaningful element in a character's life, but because we're looking for a way to survive the writing of the story. When in doubt, include things. We may have Doris over the sink trying to get the lid off the espresso maker while not getting water on the sleeves of her silk blouse, and we may not know her state of mind, but at least we have that small appliance, the running water, and her sleeves to help us into the next sentence.

3. Character is action.

Action has a bad name right now, as it's being equated with tough guys who eat nails for breakfast, spend the midday manually subduing bad guys and all of their ordnance, and sleep on rocky ground with an Uzi for a pillow and one eye open. Who doesn't know what he'll do tomorrow when they send in the helicopters. There's always helicopters. Well, not always. More telling perhaps might be what he'll do next time he's home, and a young girl comes to the door selling magazine subscriptions. We're looking for the small acts that reveal character.

Action is narrative evidence. It proves as it goes, whereas

adjectival telling (she was careless, manipulative, compulsive, willful) alerts us to how a character might be, but doesn't prove it with the force good drama requires. How many kinds of careless are there? Just over a jillion. Which was she? Show us a woman in the shower with her hair standing in a column of soapsuds who thinks about what to plan for dinner and realizes she's left her children at the beach. That's a different careless woman than the one who never once in all her thirty years closed the fridge door, and the woman who had a Scrabble game missing six letters, two E's, the K, a B, an O, and an N. She will not replace that game and insists on playing, is happy to play, with an incomplete game; she's blissful, at ease.

In a story much narrative evidence concerning character appears in exposition, that is, in periods of time before the current story. Flashbacks. In the current story we see a young woman crossing a river on a big yellow horse. Will she make it? That part, the outer story: girl, horse, river is fun to write, and we already know that we need to stay close and learn what we can, being particular about the moments in a way that is utterly convincing. But who is she? The importance of whether she makes it across the river or not will be determined by narrative evidence from the past. That's what the past is: evidence. A girl simply riding a yellow horse for the pure pleasure of it on a spring day is in one kind of jeopardy; a girl riding toward her boyfriend's house to tell him about her brand-new pregnancy is in another; and a girl who has a pistol in her pocket is in another. What is the true weight of the jeopardy? That will be determined by the way the simple narrative moments in exposition are set out, so we find out who the girl is. Not all girls, not all boys (nor all women, men, children, dogs, horses, birds, reptiles, etc.), arrive at the current moment as equals. And the way they are different is established in expository narrative evidence. Sometimes this evidence is implied, and sometimes it is presented with simple flashback scenes.

One further example of this model: a boy is waiting in an airport for the arrival of his girlfriend. He gets a coffee and a copy of the *Times*. You can do a great deal with the coffee, the plastic seat in which he tries to get comfortable, the *Times*, the other people at Gate 21, the big dirty windows, and all the inventory of such a space. You'd stay close to find out what was going on. Perhaps you can imply that he, the boy Mickey, has been at this gate for thirty-six hours straight waiting for the one thing that makes his life worth living: Doris. Perhaps you can imply that he's still warm from the toasty and kinetic bed of Cora where he was exercising so pleasantly only twenty-five minutes before. Or perhaps you will use a short paragraph somewhere early in this little story to show scenes from A or B. These flashbacks would require the same particularity and attention to inventory that the current scene, Gate 21, requires, and they—regardless if they were two or twenty lines or more—would have their own dramatic force. The story of Mickey's wait would ultimately take its power from the meeting of the two narratives. Doris would arrive or would still be out there in a holding pattern, but something would be revealed about the Mickey we've created.

going over to her window

SO CODY ARRIVES, AND I'M PLEASED about it because I know
I'm going to get another little scene. I don't know what it
will be, but I'll stay and find out. It's early in my writing day
and I've written three sentences and there's more to come.
Somewhere ahead of me I still have that mattress dropping
off the truck, and it feels like a dollar in my pocket. And now
I hit the quotation-mark key and write this dialogue:

§   "You're a mess," she said. "Is the plumber
through?"

"Done and gone. We can move back in tomorrow afternoon."

"We've got the ball in two hours."

"Okay."

"Could we not be late for once," Cody said.
It was the first time I had stood still all day, and I
felt how wet my feet were; I wanted to fight, but
I couldn't come up with anything great. "I've got
your clothes and everything. Come along."

"No problem," I said, grabbing the old rope off
the cab floor.

"You're not going to take that to the dump
now, are you?"

"Cody," I said, going over to her window,

I like that *going over to her window,* it's exactly the kind of
phrase that helps. How? By being the next thing, the physical

thing that will help me find out what—exactly—he's going to say. We don't know the precise purpose or the precise outcome of any scene of dialogue and sometimes, as we commence, we're not sure of the temperaments or agendas of the characters. We write the scene to find out. There is a great deal written about the "writing of dialogue," and I'm going to add a little to it here, but it is key to understand that it is not a simple craft problem. It is as much about process and discovery as it is about technique. You are listening to the characters, and you must sit in both (or all three or four) chairs. The writing of dialogue is certainly one of the human activities that again requires that strange thing: empathy. It is about occupying both hearts, and it is as much about how people don't listen as it is about how they might speak. In my brief section I'm simply trying to let one thing lead to another: Cody's arrived as he's finished loading the truck. He feels, though it is only a shadow in the text (though I *feel* it as I'm writing), misunderstood or underappreciated or some other off-kilter thing, and so I simply remember he has a body, and he goes over to her window. I can't wait to see what he says. Will it be: "Oh, okay, dear, I'll lock the house and come right along."

Not quite.

Let's go stand in his cold shoes for a moment and then let him speak.

writing dialogue

THE SINGLE THING I SAY the most to writers of dialogue is *slow down*. I actually don't see much clunky dialogue, but I see a lot of scenes that are too brisk, too summarily done. A writer arrives at the scene where Doris is going to leave Mickey or where Mickey has big bad news for Doris, and the writer buzzes through it, hurrying to the "Take this job and shove it!" or "You can't fire me, I quit!" or "You can fix your own dinner, you savage!" The scene had a point, and it became the characters' responsibility to deliver it, just as if they had been hired by the author out of central casting to get the job done. The thinking is that dialogue serves story the way a wheel serves a car; it is simply meant to advance the story. I'm not at all sure dialogue is meant to advance the story; I know that sometimes it is the story. There isn't anything, not a thousand-word description of the winter wind in the bare brittle elm tops or a girl worrying that the other kids at school will see that her lunch includes homemade bread, or a welder smoking a cigarette in a metal culvert, that doesn't advance the story. Since I don't know where I'm going, why would I hurry? Secondly, "advance the story" sounds like dialogue is subservient, an instrument like the trombone in a band, and that the meat of the matter is elsewhere. This is an odd metaphor, but I think the band serves the trombone as much as vice versa. I want to say story is meant to advance the dialogue; more frequently than I would even list, the heart of the story is shown most clearly in the dialogue. So don't hurry.

And in the process of writing dialogue, remember: your characters can't advance the story because *they may not know it yet.* That is a reason to slow down, listen, find out. You may have started the scene with the intention of the two characters having a quarrel and breaking up, but as you occupy the scene, it may open in another—truer—way. In genre fiction, or fiction where plot rules the characters, each of these scenes has a purpose, and we hear people talk the way they do in movies ("Get dressed, we gotta get outta here before the cops come.") We write dialogue closely, listening to how the characters invite and obstruct communication.

It's like playing tennis against a real partner who is just a little better than you are. *It is not like playing tennis against a wall.* When I hit a ball into the practice wall, I know by the velocity, angle, and height where it will return, and I can go quickly to that spot and hit it again. When you are fully involved in writing a scene where there is dialogue, again and again, you've got to let people say what the moment asks of them, and though you may have had a nifty response all at the ready, you're going to have to let it go, and have the other character respond with a word or deed that is true for them *now.*

Too often two characters act like two agents sent in by the author to "advance the story," and not like people with hopes and fears of their own.

"When we find the money, we're going to blow this town."
"That's the ticket, Jake! We'll be outta here."
"And we'll be laughing all the way to the bank."
"Jake, I'll be laughing way past the bank."

Also, the idea of one character in a scene being a back-board for someone else's news can be fraudulent. The idea of one character listening with every fiber of her being is worth challenging. No one is standing still; everyone has an agenda. Writing dialogue is about observing closely what is on each character's mind and how willing and how able he or she is to share it. And it is about observing closely how exactly people are unable or unwilling to listen to each other. In that tennis match, when you hit the ball across the net, say a low crosscourt backhand, you've got to run around the net and play as aggressive a shot as you can right back, a shot that is congruent with the force of that character's agenda (wants, fears, concerns).

One character may have just a) been fired, or b) discovered she is pregnant, or c) received an invitation to the White House; but this doesn't mean that the other characters in the scene won't have their own news, their own lives that will filter in, color the scene, and finally give it the authenticity and credibility we're looking for.

"Look, Janey, I've been invited to tea at the White House!"

"And I suppose you want to wear my red sweater."

This doesn't diminish the news, but it honors Janey by making her credible.

Taking all these craft considerations separate from story is artificial, a simple construct I'm using to focus and illuminate some of the evidence we use when writing stories. Rarely does a writer sit up straighter in her chair, shake her hands above the keyboard while she says, "Now the dialogue!" and dive back into her story. What happens is that a character, having plunged down the crumbling concrete stairs of the Fourteenth Street Subway stop and having missed the train by a car, stops and buttons his huge overcoat and turns to the female police officer there on the platform and starts talking. Or Mickey closes the silverware door with his hip, takes the bowl of pasta to the table, and as he's arranging the trivet, Doris says, "Don't use that one," which is the closest she can physically come to asking him to move out.

What is powerhouse about dialogue is that it is the one time in all your writing when your characters stand alone, unvarnished by your interpretation, and what they say, direct dialogue, can be the most potent evidence in fiction. You can write the sentence, *The four men played pool for an hour,* sixty different ways if not a hundred and sixty. But when Mickey sinks the twelve ball with a tricky combination and stands before shooting again and says, "Look, Ed, I saw Doris hitchhiking out the Beeline Highway this afternoon. What's that about?" That is what Mickey said, and we all hope after writing a line of dialogue that it doesn't go *clunk.* If you're standing there with Mickey in a room in your head with a pool table and the three other men, including Ed, then you'll be listening, and there is no chance for a wooden or ungainly phrase. If you know your character you will nail the line; if you don't, there is a chance that he or she will sound like a character in a book, meaning a *genre* book. "This town isn't big enough for the both of us." "You got us into this; you get us out." "We're meant for each other." "I'm dying, Vicky." Booky dialogue is for good and bad guys, characters that have a thin chance of getting into our stories.

One impulse that must always be resisted is the impulse to leap back in and qualify Mickey's statement with he *moaned* or he *sighed* or he *said with concern in his voice* or he with some other of the jillion modifiers available to us. Don't do it.

Most of the time (98.5 percent) what is said equals how it is said. This frees us from trying to nudge what our characters say this way or that, and it makes it imperative that we listen to what they say and write it exactly.

When we talk about dialogue, everyone thinks *talk*, when in fact that may represent a small portion of your scene. Let's think of dialogue as a physical thing, a dance. Let's think of a stage scene. Two people in one space. What forces are keeping their bodies apart? What forces are urging their bodies together? (There are always both, *though not in equal measure.*)

§   "Cody," 1 said, going over to her window, "1 just loaded this. If 1 leave it on the truck tonight, one of the tires will go flat, and you'll have to help me unload this noxious residue tomorrow so 1 can change it. I've got to go. I'll hurry. You just be ready."

That's his speech. It'll work for now. I'm still typing. What I don't see and won't for a year or so is that I've just typed his code in that sentence: "I've got to go." This guy has a strange sense of duty and is using it to avoid his responsibilities to the relationship. Without knowing it I've rigged him to work from this bad-faith position. But this is key: he doesn't know it. And I, sitting there typing in the first hour of the day, don't know it. I don't need to know. It will teach me.

Then I wrote this simple scene-ending paragraph:

§   Her window was up by the time 1 finished and 1 watched her haul the sharp black car

>   around and wheel into traffic. Since the pipes
>   had frozen, we were staying with Dirk and Evan.

Dirk and Evan: who? I don't know. I don't know any Dirk and I didn't know any Evan. At least he wasn't Mickey. There was a Dirk's Cleaners on Seventh East in Salt Lake, and I surely pinched the name from the sign. But who are they? Now, I don't care. They're placeholders. The reason I'm going on like this is that it is key to find a phrase or a name and then live with it. What am I going to do, push back from the table and stand up defeated? I don't know who these guys are. I made that up. I better go get some coffee. No, rather this: that's right—we were staying with Dirk and Evan. Count on it. That's my story and I'm sticking to it. I think I'll just stay right here and keep typing.

coffee

EVERY DAY THAT I WRITE, all these days since I wrote "The Governor's Ball," I have come to a moment early where I wanted to leave the room. No one among us suffers the radical appreciation for coffee that I do. It calls to me, but I have learned not to listen. *All the valuable writing I've done in the last ten years has been done in the first twenty minutes after the first time I've wanted to leave the room.* Although I'm perfectly willing and certainly able to overstate things in this text, I am not overstating that. I look up from the page or the screen and I think, hey, I want some coffee. There's my cup right there, just like yours, half full of cold coffee, and I'd like a cup of coffee. But now, I'll tell the truth: I've come to a little place in the story where I'm not sure of what to do; there's some decision here that I'm not fully comfortable making; in short, I want to leave the room and see what's happening in the rest of the house. I've even had this thought: maybe I'll be smarter in the other room. Somehow, I have learned to sit still for those critical twenty minutes, pushing through.

The most amazing thing about all this was that after I began to stick it out, to stay in the room, when I did finally close down the section or find a place past the tough going where I could stop, the coffee tasted so much better than it ever had before. It was then that I began to see how good coffee could be.

the outer story

I TALK A LOT WITH MY STUDENTS in workshops about what I call the outer story, what it is and what it can lead you to. That's why I focus on it as a teacher and why I live in it as a writer. The outer story is the world of the story, the real concrete elements and places of the story that is composed of all the sensory imagery. It is the evidence that will convince us that the story could actually happen. If it is the cold cab of a pickup truck in a western city, then we need to select and then illustrate the imagery necessary to prove that. If it is the argon-rich atmosphere of Dwindgore, ghost planet and county seat of Bilz, where the translucent ground glows and emits soft sparks as you walk barefoot toward the large turquoise nurturing towers, then it needs to be drawn real so we can participate in the story of the star-crossed lovers you're about to tell. The outer story is written closely, left foot—right foot, as one thing leads to another, and writing the outer story is the easy part of any story. The bear chases the boy up the Ponderosa (real bear, rough bark, lost hat, scratched wrist, breathing, vibration, etc.); a sophomore drops her tray in the cafeteria (wet plastic tray, overloaded chef salad, crash of plate, spray of dressing on ankles, etc.); after midnight a woman and her elderly father fix a tire beside the isolated two-lane that crosses the forested top of Feather Mountain (chill, heft and smell of tire, sounds of car, texture of ground for jack, stubborn lug nuts, etc.). Writing our way through an event is a straightforward activity, the goal is to keep things clear (appropriate to tone and character), and to watch what unfolds so that we can know where to put the next foot. If anything, as we explore a scene, we want to take more time than is perhaps necessary. There is no hurry to get to the point of the story; this is the point of the story. Writing the outer event is a pleasure, but it needs to be written with full attention and *done with the hands on the wheel* or we could slip quickly into the ruts of all those writers ahead of us, those who have covered similar terri-tory before—and there are some deep ruts where the traffic has been the thickest. Scenes we frequently see, such as the hospital-room visit, the homecoming, the sex scene (heavy petting scene, kissing, touching hands in a public place, seeing each other across a room, crowded or otherwise), looking in the mirror scene, falling off a horse scene, wak-ing in a cold dorm room from a warm dream scene, taking a shower when the water's cold and the soap hard to find scene, accidental death of Uncle Eugene by tractor scene, childbirth, blind date approaching porch scene, etc., etc. I had a little fun here to make the point that there are writers who have gone before. They have pushed over outhouses on Halloween, sat in the judges' quarters during divorce pro-ceedings, been assaulted, entered casinos, and stepped acci-dentally into icy streams. For us this is not caution, this is relief. It doesn't deter us in the least. Someone has written a scene where the middle-aged housewife appraises her naked body in the bathroom mirror, and now the housewife in our story steps out of the tub and looks at herself. She might. How are you going to handle it? Closely. Writing the outer story is a matter of sending yourself on the journey, send-ing yourself through the moment to find the new thing in it. Most often in the mirror scenes, the men and women think something like, "Well, still pretty good for my age." And they take some part of their body and hoist it to where it used to be. What should your character do? You find out by watching closely.

In working with writers, one of the things I've been saying a lot in these past years is: solve all your problems through the physical world. That is, if you have a scene that's stalled or muddled, go back into it carefully and write the next thing that happens in real time. Don't think, but watch instead: occupy. Many times a story will get twisted when a writer knows where she wants to go, what irony or point she wants the story to achieve, and she's got her eye on that goal and she can't see or hear the opportunities that are arising in the current scene. She knows she wants Mickey to come back in the final scene to apologize, and when he arrives at her condo after driving the fifteen hundred ragged miles from his new job in Cincinnati, she comes to the door in her silk bathrobe, hands him the same bottle of Champagne he gave her in the second scene and the same flowers (now limp but still pretty) he gave her in scene three and she tells him she's not alone and never will be again and by the way, *good-bye*. End of story. Well, maybe. When this writer was cranking out a draft, she knew she wanted that moment of revenge, and there's a chance such knowing hurried her through the curves of the story, moments that might have illuminated character and world and maybe have led the story elsewhere. Do we want a story to go elsewhere? Absolutely: *elsewhere is our destination.* We want the story to be true. We don't want it to have a point, theme, doctrine. If we write the story well, those things will emerge—we can't prevent it.

Outer story is event, and event is there to serve and amplify and reveal character. This simply means that the trials your people confront will illuminate who they are; we'll read a book to find out what happens; and we need to believe what happens so that the characters have a place and a scene in which to live. I draw event as a big cauldron on the blackboard, and then I put a couple of characters in it and show that the cauldron is boiling. My sketches confuse my students, but the ideas don't.

Character serves event in genre fiction. They hold up the plot points like banners and march them around. In the best stories, we read to tease out what happened to whom, not just what happened. Character, the human heart, is paramount in the best stories, and the human heart is a complicated and evolving organ. It is not a single thing that reacts a single way. In genre fiction (romance, western, adventure, etc.), the action is commanding and compelling, but the hearts are half drawn. People are good or bad (sometimes evil). They represent only part of us. Sometimes an appealing or fascinating part, but only part.

I've been reading stories where we're going along fine, as if traveling in a car say at forty miles per hour along a road we've never seen before, and suddenly the writer realizes his intended destination IS RIGHT OVER THERE! And with little warning and no braking, he wheels the entire mechanism ninety degrees to the left, sending the reader and all the inventory and evidence of his story smacking into the door, which hurts.

Your story is a vehicle of a certain weight and velocity. It makes every sense to obey the laws of physics and turn gently if at all. You must earn your turn. That feeling, when you think you were at the wheel of a story, in charge, and suddenly you're going by your very goal, the poignant point you wanted to make, your irony, your theme, your destiny, my god, there'll be no way you could haul everything you've created so far to that place, well, *good*. Let's lean back and see what happens next.

Outer story, the physical world, is also its own effect, its own reaction, its own comment. Outer story shows us things, and as the outer story grows and gathers, we can begin to see the constellations of our meanings. There is no need to comment on each facet of a scene. The sunset went from yellow to purple in a moment, and Jonathan took at step back, stunned. (Cut stunned.) The sunset went from yellow to purple in a moment, and I thought it was fabulous. (You know what to cut.) I've heard people talk about this by quoting Sergeant Friday: "Just the facts, ma'am." This is apt, but there's more for the writer: this frees us from having to interpret. Our mission is to write the physical scene as closely as we can, knowing that our intentions lie just beyond our knowing. Write, don't think.

"The Governor's Ball" is almost all outer story. There is very little exposition, and I'll address this later as a potential weakness of the story.

As I was sitting there that morning writing "The Governor's Ball," I realized with great relief that now for a paragraph or two I would load the truck, follow the outer story. I still had the mattress drop in my pocket, so I was fine.

i was still typing

I was still typing:

§   The old Ford was listing hard to the right rear, so I skipped back into the house for a last tour. Except for the sour water everywhere, it looked like I had everything. Then I saw the mattress. I had thrown the rancid king-size mattress behind the door when I had first started and now as I closed the front of the house, there it was. It was so large I had overlooked it. Our original wedding mattress. It took all the rest of my anger and some of tomorrow's strength to hoist it up the stairs and dance it out the back, where I levered it onto the hood of the truck by forcing my face, head, and shoulders into the ocher stain the shape of South America on one side. Then I dragged it back over the load, stepping awkwardly in the freezing carpet

The rear tire was even lower now, so I hustled, my wet feet sloshing, and tied the whole mess down with the rope, lacing it through the little wire hoops I'd fashioned at each corner of the truck bed.

This is simple. This is a breeze. I'm a typing fool. Events are wonderful to write as we follow steps in the procedure. I want it all to be real. My goal is to load the truck and tie it down and have it all believable. I've learned that if I stay close, if I stay in my narrator's mind, then something else will happen that I've already alluded to: the outer story will inform the inner story.

If you've got two guys cruising the aisles in a supermarket some Tuesday night, we'll be able to get a great deal of information about them by what they put in the basket (inventory) and how they physically pull it off the shelf and place it in their cart. A character is what he or she does.

WRITING EXERCISE: Write a 400-word scene in which one person washes a car. The person can move the car once (from the street to the driveway or the driveway to lawn, etc.), and the person can wax the vehicle if you want. You must stay with the physical story, the inventory and the actions, and you must not relate any of the character's thoughts. This will feel difficult, constrained, but it is possible. The character should emerge through the constellation of her/his actions—his/her code. You will feel the pull of history/exposition: how/when those bugs got on the windshield; the empty beer cans in the backseat, the rip in the upholstery, the origin of the three gold coins, the rusty knife, etc. But: be strict, just the facts. This will help you measure how much you can leave out and how powerful what you include actually is.

So, I feel lucky, writing along about loading the truck, because I can do that and because I know I still have some driving ahead of me. I don't have to quit, yet, admit failure, and go out and vacuum the living room.

§   There was always lots of play in the steering of the Ford, but now, each time it rocked backward, I had no control at all. My fingers were numb and the truck was so back-heavy that I careened down Fifth South like a runaway wheelbarrow. The wind had really come up now, and I could feel it lifting at me as I crossed the intersections. It was cold in the cab, the frigid air crashing through the hole where the radio had been, but I wasn't stopping. I'd worried my way to the dump in this great truck a dozen times.

bloomfield avenue

NOTHING NOVEL HERE. Simply a strange truck on a cold day—oh, I did introduce the wind so it can eat the mattress later. Fifth South, as I said earlier, is the real street in Salt Lake. All the addresses are real addresses in this story. Why? For authenticity? No. If they offer some authenticity (a word with the same root as author), great, but I set my story on the real streets because it helped me write the story. Whenever I haven't known the name of a street and I wanted to be specific, I've used "Bloomfield Avenue"—and it took me years to type that and believe it. My impulse after writing, "...I careened down Bloomfield Avenue like a runaway wheelbarrow," was to write, "No I didn't, there's no truck, and Bloomfield Avenue? I made that up." My goal, my entire reason for being, on this morning when I'm typing "The Governor's Ball," is to keep typing. I don't want to get caught up in all the city planning necessary to create a world for my story. That would be just asking to stop typing. Luckily I've got a city and I know it pretty well. And I'll use it as a scaffold to reach the various cornices of my story, and if it is only in the story because it is real and has no other value, then I can cut it later. I've done that in stories, and so have you. I'm very good at writing five thousand words to get four thousand. But for now: Fifth South. (When I wrote the story, "Keith,"—also set in Salt Lake City—I used "Bloomfield Avenue" and let it stand. In that story, "Bloomfield Avenue" is really *Fourth* South.) There are a lot of streets in "The Governor's Ball"—Twenty-first South, Ninth West, Fourth

South, etc., and they are all real. And they all helped. As a writer I could stand on them so that my character could drive over them. That is the purpose of the designated highways and biways—to help us finish our stories, to help us get where we didn't know we were going.

now i'm at a critical juncture

NOW WOULD BE A GREAT TIME for a cup of coffee. I've finished this section of outer story, and I might be able to do some better thinking out in the kitchen with Mr. Coffee and Mr. Refrigerator, and oh, there in the other room is Mr. Television, and there's Mr. Bed. And others. No, we won't go there.

the inner story

THE OUTER STORY IS THE MOTOR of your story, and the inner story is the freight. The outer story becomes a convincing vicarious experience for the reader, drawing the reader far enough into the story for you to have your way with him or her. We read to find out what happened and end up caring about those who were affected by the event. Let me say that so it's useful to us: we write to find out what happened and—if we're careful about that discovery process, typing with true attention—then we end up creating real characters worthy of belief. The inner story is always about the complicated interplay of the facets of the human heart. In the best stories it is irreducible to a phrase. The outer story can be summed up in those two lines for *TV Guide:* "Jill washes her husband's pickup and comes to terms with the future." Oh? She does? Does "coming to terms" mean "find words for"? She may, but it would be a mistake to make our characters too capable of understanding and articulating their own condition. Our job in the outer story is to create a real truck, a real bucket of suds, a heavy wet rag (the corner of an old towel), the smell of water on the warm cement driveway, Jill in her cutoffs, her hair tied back with a big red plastic clip. These things need to be convincing. They need to be convincing *to the writer,* so that he or she can have a place to stand to write the next sentence. Only in simplistic stories would Jill suddenly "realize" or "come to understand" some clear thing: she did/didn't love Rick; she wanted a baby; she'd never been close to another human being; she'd been a hideous wife; she'd been lying to herself all these years about being happy as a dental hygienist. Stories that go night-to-day this way are melodramatic, and they deny our real human complexity. Certainly, in "The Governor's Ball," the main character is capable of coping, but not capable of declaring—for the convenience of the reader—exactly what is bothering him or where he is headed. Literature is one place where we honestly acknowledge and sometimes celebrate how imprecise an instrument the human being is when it comes to registering and measuring the true ramifications of life on earth.

I'm still wandering *into* this draft of my story. I like to think that way, that all you have to do is write your way into the event deeply enough so that getting out will be a struggle; you're going to make a mess, spill something, reveal more than you knew you intended. In writing "The Governor's Ball," I'm not worried about my "freight," the inner story. I'm going to trust (and hope) that if I'm careful in writing about vehicles, the weather, and the next physical thing, that the contours of my inner story will emerge.

That's all developing; meanwhile I haven't even lost the mattress yet. So, in my wandering toward that event, I type a short paragraph *away* from the outer story.

§   The Governor's Ball is two hundred dollars per couple, but we went every year as Dirk's guests. The event itself is held at the Hotel Utah, and the asparagus and salmon are never bad, but holding a dress ball in January is a sort of mistake, all that gray cleavage, everyone sick of the weather.

Facts. Exposition. I was surprised to find out who Dirk was, and in fact as I typed that I realized who the real person was on whom I was basing this shadowy character. Good, I'm glad I got some use out of him, and immediately upon adopting him, he starts to shift into whatever the story might require.

what is left out

"THE GOVERNOR'S BALL" IS A STORY with minimal exposition; there's very little information about these people's past histories. Most conventional stories (which is what I'm addressing here), in fact, have more backstory, exposition—the facts that came before the current moment. Minimal fiction celebrates the moment and offers little of this context, and the complaint about it many times was that while we could understand the scene before us, we couldn't decipher to whom it mattered. And sometimes the event of the story was so quiet, so utterly poker-faced and still, that it was difficult to perceive what exactly had happened, let alone what the consequences were for whom. When these stories "work"— that is when there is just enough data for us to apprehend the contours of the story that are suggested by what's on the page, they have power. They scare and affect us like letters about people we know, and their terrific efficiency makes them that much more affecting and smart.

The assumption on the part of any writer that she is writing about people we all know (without explanation) is a useful one. It's called not underestimating your audience; readers are terribly smart. It's a relief and allows us to leave things out. Minimalism was the simple response to the kind of fiction that overexplained, drowning us in cloying evaluations of things we already knew. There is a balance wherein necessary history is implied or stated, and so the voltage in the outer story is clear. Many times we achieve or work on this balance in the rewrite.

As is apparent already, I'm not trying as a writer to be smart or to understand the inner workings of my narrator, I'm trying to survive the typing of this story. I can only be smart from *time to time,* and that phrase has nothing to do with being a writer. So, I'm just pressing on, not discriminating as to what to exclude. If it pops up in my way, it goes in. I've got later (with the help of the teacher, editor, critic, reader) to pare and to amplify. In other words: I can be smart later.

Although I'm getting a little worried because as I started writing this story I had dropped a big piece of furniture, and now I'm approaching that moment. It's a bit like being lost in the woods and reaching in your pocket as darkness thickens in the trees and putting your cold hand on your last lemon drop. That's dinner, and if you don't do something, it'll be breakfast too. I don't want to perish on this trip.

§   I was thinking about how Dirk always seated himself by Cody, how he made sure she was taken care of, how they danced the first dance, when the light at Third West turned green and I mounted the freeway.

Now there's a two-part sentence! I liked the first half because it was a little leap; there it is—a suggested dynamic between Dirk and Cody. And I use the second half to do what I've been doing all along: follow the *outer story* of the event.

§   As soon as I could, I squeezed way right to get out of everybody's way, and because the wind here was fierce, sheering across at forty miles per hour, at least. The old truck was rocking like a dinghy; I was horsing the steering wheel hard, trying to stay in my lane, when I felt something go.

Now here, when something is happening "suddenly," I tend to slow down. Instead of writing, "Boom! The garage exploded!" I'd prefer to see: "Mickey stepped out of the taxi and put his suitcase on the driveway. There were no birds in the sycamores behind the house. Something was funny. As he pulled the folded bills from his pocket to pay the driver, the garage lifted, the whole thing coming at him . . ." We'll put the boom—or its equivalent—down a sentence or two. Part of this also is that I'm reluctant to spend all my money, use the last thing I know. It's going to take me two or three phrases for the mattress to vanish:

§   There was a sharp snap and in the rearview mirror I saw the rope whip across the back. The mattress rose like a playing card and jumped up, into the wind. It sailed off the truck, waving over the rail, and was gone. I checked the rear, slowing. The mattress had flown out and over and off the ramp, five stories to the ground. I couldn't see a thing, except that rope, snapping, and the frozen carpet which wasn't going anywhere.

The main reason I took a moment with this little action is that I'm dragging my feet. I don't exactly know what is going to happen next, and so I extend the mattress's exit to see if I can figure something out. I could take a moment now and talk about the wonderful power a fiction writer has over time, how he can go into slow or fast motion as it serves him, making a shave last forty pages, eating an apple for seven thousand words, an entire three-year stint in the military in a ten-word phrase, but I won't. When I play with time it's because I'm trying to stay in the room, get something right. But the manipulation of time (which often becomes an important instrument when considering a second draft) is one of the primary acknowledgments of the vast chasm between words and deeds; and how much time something gets, how many lines of prose that is, is a clear indicator of the kind of subjectivity (and many times *tone, point of view*) that you want to project.

WRITING EXERCISE: Take a simple act, say unbuttoning a shirt, tying a tie, pulling on a sock, pouring a cup of coffee, removing a sliver from a finger, etc., and write it in slow motion, that is, give it two hundred words. Don't automatically lapse into hyperbole (and thereby the comic), but think of the effect: make it sensuous, matter-of-fact, sinister, gross, comic, etc. Or: take an event that takes a season, a year, a couple of years, an era, an epoch, etc., and write it in a phrase or a sentence. "Myra had four children in a row, turned twenty-six, and stood in the hall window with both hands over her mouth."

By now in "The Governor's Ball," I'm terrified. I've done all the easy stuff, written my little event following the outer story as best I could, the way you'd follow a marked trail through the forest, and I've come to the end of that trail and I feel a lot like standing up and heading out to the kitchen, which is to say like lying down there in the woods until grim death lays his cold hands on me. But I have one more little crumb in my knapsack, that is, I know I continued to the landfill, so I can write that tiny episode and then lie down and wait for <u>gruesome</u> failure to grace me with his icy touch.

§   The traffic all around me slowed, cautioned by this vision. I tried to wave at them as if I knew what was going on and everything was going to be all right. At the Twenty-first South exit, I headed west, letting the rope snap freely, as if whipping the truck for more speed.

That's all I can do. Is it great? No. But it is that other blessed thing: serviceable. It is writing that takes me in its way from one place to another. Quite simply, it is the next thing. It serves—I'm still alive. I have had the opportunity to quit, and I have declined. For now. I was still in the room. I continued in this fashion:

§   The dump, lying in the lea of the Kennecott tailings mound, was strangely warm. Throwing the debris onto the mountain of trash, I could smell certain sweet things rotting, and my feet warmed up a bit. By the time I swept out the truck, it was full dark. I still had half an hour to make the Governor's Ball.

the clock is on the field

I STILL HAD half an hour to make the Governor's Ball is my way of regrouping, reminding us all of the purpose of this quest and offering a sense of time pressure. In certain stories, that sense, that the clock is ticking, is a way of keeping a dramatic pressure through the piece. It's the equivalent of those last two minutes in a lacrosse game when the timer steps onto the playing field holding the big clock.

inventory

I'VE BEEN TYPING for about an hour now and it feels as if I've exhausted what I know, what I had. I'm certain that I'm not going to type out what happened; I *want* this story to take off, and I want to see what is going to happen to my character. My credo is: just follow, approach the unknown with simple knowns, stay in the physical world, figure what *could be earned* by what has gone before. The notion that my writing day or my story will be solved by something from the outside, something I think up, make up, dream up, something that comes over the far hill of my life like the advancing cavalry or a killer tornado or a young woman in sheer lingerie carrying a candle (though there are fine places in fine stories for such things—when they are earned) is wrongheaded. I'm staying in the room to allow something to emerge. Most of the ingredients necessary to the story should be in place by the two-thirds mark. No new inventory—nothing that hasn't been suggested by something that has come before—after that point.

Teachers often speak of reading as a writer, and it usually means reading closely, reading to understand the writer's choices. It involves imaginative speculation. I sometimes ask my students to read a story this way:

When reading a story, mark the two-thirds point with a pencil. Stop reading at that place and make an inventory of the story: characters, sets, events in progress, etc. If you'd written this far with these things, how would you close? How does your writer's projection compare to what the writer did? Are there significant new elements introduced after the two-thirds point?

The companion writing exercise obviously goes like this:

When writing a story based and centered on a single event, stay close to the physical world, closer than the real details. Don't plan or project, try to learn from what you've written, what you should write next. Listen closely, write closely, simply trying to evoke the real world of your story.

potshots

NOW I'M AT A TURNING POINT in my story, literally. I'm as far away from home with this guy as he's going to get, and starting back gives me even more reason to pause. I still have not discovered what this story might be about. I like the few pages I've achieved, but as we all know the world is glutted with magnificent three-page starts, and the road to hell is paved with unfinished manuscripts. This all makes me slow down.

§   I hit it hard driving away from the dump, just like everybody does, hoping to blow the microscopic cooties from their vehicles, but when I got back to Ninth West, I turned off. I didn't want to go retrieve the mattress; it was nine years old and had been in the basement three. But I had lost it. I had to call Cody.

I regret that one phrase, "microscopic cooties." It's a little joke. I was imagining driving away from the landfill, and it popped up and I nabbed it (as I should in a first draft—if something occurs, it gets in), but I should have cut it later. It's too cute for my context here and isn't really worth it, a little sideshow. But the rest of the paragraph serves me well. He states his agenda as, "I didn't want to go retrieve the mattress," and then I made up some history, which by this time in the story I can believe even though it is total air, and then I listened to him. *I had to call Cody.*

That last sentence creates a door. I'm probably going to get to write a phone call, another little scene. But what will it be, and when, and where will it lead? My responsibility is to follow, not to lead.

I know Ninth West in Salt Lake City and have had some adventures near there, but I did not go there the day I dropped the mattress. But I can believe that it would be on Ninth West where a person would drop off the expressway and look for a phone. I wrote this before cell phones were ubiquitous—and, when pay phones were a dime! And what we are trying to engender and foster with each sentence is the writer's belief. So now I'm about to make something up, as we say, but it's not much of anything because it is based on experiences that naturally, by association, are suggested by the street, the place I am in the story.

the purpose of a scene

ONE OF THE LITTLE TRICKS I'll pull in class sometimes is to stop the discussion of the story at hand and say, "Let's imagine there's been some good news; we've been hired to make a film of this story. Someone quickly give me the number of scene setups we'll need." We list them and then determine which seem more significant. The exercise becomes a way of scanning a story for dramatic possibility. Many times it reveals that there are fewer concrete scenes than the story is going to need to have its way. Do we know when and where we are? Is the place established in such a way that we believe it? What is the inventory of the place?

The lawyer's office, the barn, the new-car showroom, all require concrete imagery to convince us that something can happen. Each has an extensive inventory of sensory detail with which we are all familiar. There is the generic barn, the generic law office, the generic car showroom. There isn't anyplace we haven't already been—even the glowing caverns of Nozzlerack on the lost moon of Zard. We want to create a space, a set that has at least some fresh facet, a single radical element that will anchor the place as being real. This doesn't involve far-out thinking, though we see that from time to time in fiction, but more commonly a simple touch that transcends the generic. We don't need an elaborate hammock in the lawyer's office or twin bowling-pin lamps or an inch-thick Persian rug or a David Hockney watercolor or the bench seat from a Plymouth Fury, but we need something, the faint smell of mildew, a dying Bonsai tree, a walnut table ruined by water rings, a bowl of keys, a framed menu from the Titanic, a bricked-up window, a shirt draped over one of the chairs. Same for the barn. There, of course, we'd have something stored, a boat or a motorcycle, the smell of oil or oats, a row of dusty filing cabinets. In the new-car show-room I'd have a leak in the roof and the business, the bucket and the rags, such a situation would involve.

How important is place/setting? It is essential. As we know, *nothing happens nowhere.* The place many times *is* what will happen. And to a writer—not the reader—place is the fabric and the instrument that are going to help you find out what is going to happen. That is why we take such care to establish place as our characters move into it.

Scene is a word that speaks of unity of place, and unity of place translates many times as dramatic pressure. Things pool. Or better: things simmer, boil. I use Boyle's law—from Chemistry—many times when talking about scene: we need a container into which to put our material so we can heat it up and find out what it is made of. The container is place. If a woman goes to a remote trailhead, parks her Buick, and walks up half a mile to an abandoned campsite because she is depressed and considering desperate measures, the camp is a necessity for her extremity. A woman in a vague place may not suffer. No real camp, no mental anguish. We need that burned-out campfire, the bits of foil in the black charcoal, the log someone has hauled over to sit on, the packed dirt, the rusty nails in the spruce trunk, the view of the gorge and the long valley up from which she has driven. Contain her, and then she can boil. Without place, it is all like trying to boil water with no pan. Writers will hurry a scene because they know what is going to happen, and they don't want it to evaporate before the woman can say or do what she's going to do in this terrific moment, and those scenes read as thin linear story notes with little temperature. Slow down, include, find out

A way to establish this custom is by overdoing it:

Write a paragraph in which a character enters a space (a car, a classroom, a clinic, a kitchen, a backyard, a beach, etc.). Inventory *all* the senses of the space as she moves toward her goal (getting comfortable, finding a seat, getting a glass of water, finding the rake, etc.). Take your time. Include. What you are doing is creating a believable, "pressurized," container for the next event.

---

the bar

§   The first neon I ran across was a place called
The Oasis, a bar among all the small industries in
that district. Inside, it was smotheringly warm and
beery.

That's all. I gave the bar a name, and then as we move
inside, I use some imagery to establish the set and contrast
it with the cold. It is enough for me to believe and thereby
carry on. Although I am definitely now building one sentence on the one before it because I did not in fact go into
this place. *I have now for the first time in the writing of this
story* linked the events that actually happened with an event
that did not happen in contiguous time. This is the kind of
connection that happens all the time in stories; it is relatively
easy to step off something that happened onto something
else that kind of happened, even though it was two weeks
or twenty years earlier. There is still a "solid" base of remembered experience that we sometimes use with much more
willingness and facility than "invented" material.

As I have noted, I treated (embellished/slanted) the remembered events as well as I could, attempting to get an
angle, a spin, a distance, an intuitive understanding of them.
My through-story is my character's "quest" toward the Governor's Ball, and on that I will string events as they occured in
real life, or as they occur to me as a writer, or as they volun-
teer to be included. Now I am going to slip a different kind
of bead on my string.

§   I hadn't realized how cold my hands were until I
     tried for the dime in the pay phone. The jukebox
     was at full volume on Michael Jackson singing
     "Beat It!" so that when Cody answered, the first
     thing she said was: "Where are you?"

Her line is simply the result of sitting in her chair; she
hears the music, she asks the question. The spare dialogue
continues:

§   "I lost the mattress; I'm going to be late."
          "What?"
          "Go along with Dirk; I'll join you. Don't let
     anybody eat my salmon."
          "Where are you?"
          "The mattress blew out of the truck; I've got to
     go get it. And Cody,"
          "What?"
          "Behave."

If I look at this for non sequiturs, I can see these two people
speaking in a kind of code, the kind of code people who know
each other employ, full of fits and starts, repetition and lapses.
But in writing dialogue, all I want is for each speaker to have
an agenda—however small—and my responsibility is to occupy each heart. That last *"Behave"* is another small stroke
that hearkens to the past, and it offers a minimal exposition.
Are there other times when she hasn't behaved? Is that part of
what's going on with this guy? I don't know. I think that word
is something people have said to me. It felt good to write it, I
know, but I was worried about where I was going.

As I've noted, my guide is: <u>solve your problems with the physical world of the story</u>. Don't think. *Stay in both rooms*—the one you are creating and the one in which you're writing. Sometimes it's a hilltop, sometimes an airplane, sometimes a bar. Stay there until something happens next; it is the truest way one thing can lead to another.

Now, in my story I'm at some kind of midpoint, and I'm full of uncertainty about which way to go; a close reader will see that the next page or so will reflect this. But it was a great relief to write the next sentence, a good sentence in my opinion, a fabulous sentence for me that day, a useful bit of writing really because it opened a new door:

§ It was not until I had hung up that I saw the dancer.

What? The dancer! Who? There's a dancer in the bar. I am going to get another paragraph before I stumble down the stairs and into the kitchen. I can keep typing! I didn't know there'd be a dancer when we began, and there she is. You can imagine me using peripheral vision to find her, right? There is no hurry. Since I have no narrative goal, no ironic twist (or sincere point), nor some other clear and identifiable object toward which I am marching double-time with blinders on, I can afford to look left and right to see what might be included. And, of course, there is no more promising element to introduce into a story than a character.

§ They had built a little stage in the corner of the bar and a young girl wearing pasties and a pair of Dale Evans fringed panties was dancing to the jukebox.

Now I'm going to follow sentence by sentence.

§ Her breasts were round and high and didn't bounce
  very much, though they threw nice shadows when
  the girl turned under the light.

That may be all I'll get here, an extra in the background.
I don't know. My story seems to have stopped, but I've got to
tolerate it, *stay there:*

§ I sat in my own sour steam at the end of the bar
  and ordered a beer.

He orders a beer? Is he stalling? It feels odd for me to
type such a thing, but true too. Doesn't he have someplace
to be, something to do? I'm not sure and neither is he. I'm
letting the writing of the story influence what happens in the
story, as if there were a choice.

§ My fingernails ached as my hands warmed.

Another touch of the world, imagery. I will say here that
when I finished the story, I did go back through the entire
draft and rewrite to adjust and enhance the cold. I believe
in rewriting for one element. There are times when I don't
know how to make a story better, but I can make it colder. I
rewrote once only for temperature.

§ All the men along the row sat with their backs to
  the bar to see the girl. I sat forward, feeling the

grime melt in my clothes, and watched her in the mirror.

When the song ended, there was some applause, but only from two tables, and the lights on the stage went off.

That feels like the end of that scenario and now what? What is the inventory of the room?

§   The barmaid was in front of me and I said *no, thanks,* and then she turned a little and said, "What would you like, Terry?"

The inventory I've created includes two women, the barmaid and the dancer who now appears not as some magical surprise but because she is almost my only option. Her name I see as I type it is Terry.

§   I realized that the dancer was standing at my elbow. Now she was wearing a lacy fringed pajama top too, and I could see that she was young, there was a serious pimple above one of her eyebrows.

That pajama top and that pimple are simply character evidence, details added to help me believe the moment, so I can stay in the moment.

§   I didn't know I was staring at her until she said: "Don't even *try* to buy me a drink." I started to put up my hands, meaning I was no harm, when she

added: "I've seen your kind before. Why don't you
go out and do some good?"

Her remarks surprised me and emerged from a place
certain expressions come from when you're deep enough in
a story to start to get lost and you're listening to everything,
everybody. She's sick of being hit on by customers; she's not
in the story to facilitate my guy's evening; she's in the story
because she's got a job at this sorry bar. And when she speaks,
she speaks from *her* center. She doesn't speak to advance the
story or to serve the plot or to symbolize anything; she speaks
because she sees something in the narrator that ticks her off a
little, and she offers him a piece of her mind, not mine, not the
story's. There's more to be said about the dancer, invented ten
or fifteen minutes before her first and last lines in the story,
but I see now (not then, not while I was writing the story) that
this space, created because of the need for a phone call, offers
an oblique moment of recognition for the narrator.

What did she mean by her remarks? It is irrelevant to me
while I'm writing. What is relevant? That I believe the bar,
the barmaid, the dancer. Now I can go forward.

§   The barmaid looked at me as if I had started the
whole thing, and before I could speak, she moved
down to serve the other end.
      It was a long walk to the truck but I made it.
January. The whole city had cabin fever. She'd seen
my kind before. Not *me:* my *kind.*

Now I am nervous. I had a good run in the barroom,
typing through it and now I'm back out in the cold, in the

truck. I am out, almost out of the elements of the event: What's next? What I've been hoping is that by keeping my head down I could create a narrative with enough volume and velocity that its natural trajectory would take, carry me on toward some further point, some truer destination.

But I am nervous. I'm thinking I'd like to get some coffee. I'm thinking I'd like the phone to ring and have it be any of ten people who would call and say meet me for coffee. A little coffee here after typing for an hour or so, why not? Stretch the legs, that's it, and then while I'm in the kitchen, peek outside at the other world, see what's happening, breathe the larger air, witness the passing traffic, every car full of writers who have already given up. I'm warning myself what not to do and why not to do it. I don't want coffee: I want this story. There is no help but staying there. I want to leave the room. I will not. So I type:

§   The old truck was handling better now, and I conducted it back along Ninth West to Ninth South and started hunting. I'd never been under that on-ramp before, except for one night when Cody took me to The Barb Wire, a western bar where we watched all her young lawyer friends dance with the cowboys. In the dark, the warehouses made their own blank city. It was eight o'clock.

Ninth and Ninth are real streets though I've moved them a little, and The Barb Wire was the name of an actual place where I had been once with a friend from Alaska. Should you change the name of actual businesses? That's your call. Sometimes it's easier to change a name right on the spot and then live with it and grow used to it, believe it, but in your first draft, why ask for thinner ice? Use the name the first time through and then replace and adjust it later. I've been putting Bill and Nada's Cafe in my stories for twenty years, but always under different names. There's another issue here too: What is more fictional, some bar's name or your story? It is the sad truth that a dozen real places that I've taken as my own have gone out of business in the "real" world to have their only ongoing commerce in my little tale. Alas, The Barb Wire is long gone except for this page. As is Bill and Nada's, a real loss. Also, of course, The Barb-Wire sentence is another of the three or four in the entire story that is exposition offering a tiny look at who these people are via their history.

My tendency is to follow expositional information much further than I've done here. Let it in, find out. It is the data that will determine the value and charge of the current moment. "The Governor's Ball" could use more exposition; for example, it would have not been heavy-handed to add here: Cody and her women friends liked slumming, trading in their Nordstrom lawyer duds for tight jeans and red cowboy boots to cross over to the west side of town. They were still all players in a kind of competitive flirting game that I could see Cody wanted to join from time to time.

The aim is to say enough to imply the rest, and it is a balancing act we're playing every time we open the past in a story. The main thing to remember here is that I see that I drop into exposition when I'm trying to delay, avoid, prolong what is happening in the current story. Looking at the entire paragraph, you can see my uncertainty about what will happen. I wander here and there casting my line. After reminding us of what time it is, I try some supposition, fantasy, about what might be happening at the fund-raiser:

§ Cody and Dirk were having cocktails in the Lafayette
Suite. She'd be drinking vodka tonics with two
limes. Dirk would be drinking scotch without any
ice. He would have the Governor's elbow in his left
palm right now, steering him around to Cody, "You
remember Cody Westerman. Her husband is at the
dump."

This bit, where I leave the current story to suppose what
is going on at the reception, is a mode—though I don't know
it yet—that I'm going to use one more time before I'm finished. More to the point, I know why I did that: because
I'm nearly stumped in the current story. I'm digging for the
last crumbs of what I have. In that fix, as a writer, I cast left
and right, back and forward hoping to strike something on
which to base the next sentence. Now, with the thin ner-
vousness we all know, I'm going to creep forward, each word
at the edge of the void.

§ I crossed under the ramp at Fourth West and
weaved under it to the corner of Fifth, where I did
a broad, slow U-turn across the railroad tracks to
scan the area.

That sentence, literally, feels like the end. The day's writing is over and with the day's writing, perhaps the week's
writing, and why not the month's, the season's, the year's?
Should I let this problem of not knowing what comes next
defeat me? Many times the challenge of writing the next page
in fiction is the challenge of holding two things in mind at
the same time: what you know of the elements of an event
and what you are trying to find out. One of them is so solid

and mundane it feels like no help, and the other is so ephemeral that it won't support your weight. So here I have brought myself to the edge, the literal precipice of knowing, and I write the one-word fragment:

§   Nothing.

You can look it up; it's there in the text. Nothing. What an accurate assessment of my situation. Nothing, nothing, nothing. What is there: nothing. What is ahead: nothing. Oh god, you beautiful blank page: nothing! It is what we face by the moment: nothing. Will I finish this sentence, or will I end up lost and hovering over . . . nothing? Our passion requires we press on into this unknown thing. I hated typing that word there that day, but now, of course, I appreciate how right it was: nothing. I pressed on and wrote a sentence that made me queasy.

§   Two derelicts leaned against the back of a blue post
    -office van, drinking out of a paper sack. I cruised
    slowly up beside them.

It terrified me: Ron Carlson rips off the homeless to write his little story. The truest thing about the sentence was my native inclination: when in doubt, serious doubt, trouble, trouble at the edge of the known world, *bring in a character or two.* But now that I had let them in, I had a responsibility to them.

I've met nonfiction writers who think writing fiction is easy because of the notion, "You guys just make things up. You get in a corner, make something up. We have to stick to the facts." I appreciate that sentiment, especially the concept of the constraint of recorded or witnessed events, but the responsibility all writers have to the people in our work and to the just presentation of corollary evidence is equally compelling.

Years ago I interviewed a hardy young man who had survived a mountain-climbing disaster in Wyoming. I was writing a story about a rescue he had been part of, saving two lives that certainly would have been lost. I spent a long fall afternoon in his sunny kitchen in Jackson Hole, and when I drove away with all my notes and two cassette tapes, the oddest and most solemn feeling descended on me: I was now responsible to him. I had to report his story as fully and truly as I could. It is no different in fiction. You don't wave your hand and release two bluebirds; you don't wave your hand and release any birds at all except those that are mandated by the scene you are lost in. If I create two "derelicts," as the narrator calls these people, then I must inhabit this scene as fully as I can, listening and watching with all my powers for ways to earn them, make them real. In the prose that follows, you can sense the pace shift, slow, as I took my time—I had to—and sat in every chair.

§   "Hi, you guys," I said. It was the first time all day
      I felt fine about being so dirty. They looked at me
      frankly, easily, as if this meeting had been arranged.
      One, his shirt buttoned up under his skinny chin,
      seemed to be chewing on something. The other had
      the full face of an Indian, and I was surprised to see
      she was a woman. They both wore short blue Air
      Force jackets with the insignias missing.

With this paragraph I step into the void. This did not happen. I did not meet these two characters. "I made it up," we sometimes say. And to that phrase I say, yes and no. I'm not sure we spontaneously create anything, but rather I think we find elements of stories suggested suddenly by the context— if we've created the context, the place, the moment with credible force. So two characters enter my story, and I try to earn them back from the brink of stereotype by having them lean against a post-office truck (good), giving them a bottle in a paper sack (poor), having one chew on something (fair), the other a Native American woman (okay), and giving them both thrift-store jackets (good not great). I'm all right here, that is, it is enough for me to believe I can stand on it to write the next sentences. When you step out onto the ineffable fabric of your own invention, it is key, essential to act just like that character in the cartoons who steps off the cliff onto the absolute air. Do not look down. You wrote it; you can stand on it to reach for the next thing.

I need to add here that in the first draft, my two characters were both men and two pages from here (I'll indicate where) I wrote, "... she said ..." and I thought, that's right, it's a woman, and I went back *right then,* not later, which I would usually do, and I changed it.

§   "Have you seen a mattress?"

I did not foresee getting to write such a sentence when I began; I do not forsee what the answer will be, so I write:

§   The woman said something and turned to the man.

The entire reason, 100 percent of the reason, the total reason she speaks to the man and we don't hear is that I don't know what she is saying. Seriously, I don't know. I'm going to have to stay here for a moment and find out about these people, occupy their jackets.

Also: I cannot know that by having her speak that way, I have found the way the story will end. Look ahead at the last lines; they are spoken by her through her close associate, the man. I like the way they talk; there is something intimate and secret about their whispering, but I create it here simply and solely because as I enter the scene I do not know what the elements or the outcome of the interchange are going to be. I know our guy wants, for whatever reason, to find his mattress.

§   "What did she say? Have you seen one?"
      The man took a short pull on the bottle and
      continued chewing.

"Bottle" and "chewing" are inventory items I see from above that I can use *while I consider what this news will be.* Physical actions are not the frosting on the cake of dialogue; they are not gingerbread work on the pretty fringes of your story. The physical bodies are the instruments by which you find what might be credibly exchanged in a scene of dialogue.

§   "She said, *what kind of mattress is it?*" He passed
      the bottle to the woman and she smiled at me.

What kind of mattress is it? was a big step toward allowing these people agendas. The reason that she (through him) answers a question with a question (which is perfectly logical and utterly pervasive in American society) is that the author doesn't know the outcome of any of this; he does not know where the mattress is. I'm not going to have the woman say: *"Your mattress is right over there. Good night."* My story would be over and I'd be on my way toward some coffee shop.

§   I thought: Okay. What kind of mattress is it. Okay, I can do this. "It was a king-size Sealy Posturepedic."

This works all right: I'm being literal.

§   "King-size?"

This is simply about taking time: left foot, right foot.

§   "Yes: king-size. Have you seen it?"
      He took the bottle back from the woman and nodded at me.
      "You have? Where?"

I don't know. What will they say next? I'm out past the edge in this story trying not to look down.

§   "Would this king-size postropeeda fly out of the sky?" the man said. His eyes were bright; this was the best time he'd had all day.

I see that all the statements by the man and woman who were out drinking in the cold *are questions*. It's my way of fishing for them, trying to locate who they are, what they do, what they want. I don't know them well enough right now, having just run across them five minutes ago, to have them start making demands, assertions, statements. An agenda is what a character wants or what a character fears. Every character, as we've noted, must have an agenda. No one stands still, waits to be a receptacle for another character's news. There is no blank tablet. These two people were not out in the night waiting for my guy to drive along in his bad-faith funk so they could help him. They've been out in the cold probably because their options are narrowed. They don't have a home. A man alone (or two men) could go to the shelter, which I know for a fact to be close to where this encounter is transpiring. But a man and woman, if they decide to stay together, would hang out, loiter, default the night away. They are out in the cold because they have no place to go. They're in no hurry to help or hinder my guy; they see he's not a threat. They wait. They respond with questions.

§   "It would."

And then because I've followed the cause-effect of this dialogue to this point, I get the next line, the line that quickens me suddenly after typing for an hour because I make a solid connection. A door opens on the rest of the story, and I know now that I will survive the writing of this story because I believe in the two street people:

§   "What's it worth to you?" he said.

That's right, I thought. They have an agenda too. Now there is a dynamic established. I see what everyone wants; rather, I see that everyone wants something. (Although I'm not sure I could reduce the narrator's true desires to a paragraph; and I know he couldn't.)

At this point I can lean back into my story a bit. I'm not as worried about running out of material because this new room has opened for me, and I can explore it. If I'm careful and attentive, one thing will lead to another.

§   "Nothing, folks. I was throwing it away."
        "You threw it all right!" the woman said, and
        they both laughed.

It's a bit of a surprise to me that these two people are so relaxed, comfortable. I sometimes use the metaphor of walking into the ocean and finding that moment when your feet no longer touch. That heart-quickening moment is where I am now in the draft of this story; it is when I know I am beyond what I originally knew going in, and it is a moment I have come to look forward to. As I noted, I'm taking my time, and further, I am working explicitly against stereotype.

Working against type has led to what I call the 180-degree rule, which simply means that you introduce a character by considering the least likely things he or she may do. How can the character surprise us? If the character doesn't emerge from type, there is a good chance he/she is serving the plot in a way that may lead you to miss an opportunity to make the moment even more credible. Consider this:

Look at the draft of a story you have written in the last two months. Locate the third character introduced. What does he/she do for a living? Give it a name: executive secretary, lumberjack, waiter, information specialist. Work against type; that is, work consciously to make the character *run against* our general/typical notions of how such a person might act.

In my story these two people have—by their sense of comfort and well-being—awakened something new in me. Now I see they're in; they're in charge; they've taken over my story whether I like it or not. Now I have finally "made something up."

About such scenes, episodes, we ask: Did that *happen?* No, but I believe it enough to make it *true.*

§   I waited, one arm on the steering wheel, but then I saw the truth: these two were champion waiters; that's what they did for a living.

"Where's the mattress? Come on. Please. It's not worth anything."

Standing in the cold night in those old jackets, my characters now are capable of irony. They're playing with him.

§   "Okay, what's it worth?"

"Two bottles of this," the man said, pulling a fifth of Old Grand Dad from the bag.

"That's an expensive mattress."

The man stopped chewing and said, "It's king-size." They both laughed again.

"Okay. It's a deal. Two bottles of bourbon. Where is it?"

I don't know, but I'm in motion. I can type my way to it, and in the next paragraph I do—after a short moment:

> §   For a minute neither moved, and I thought we were in for another long inning of waiting, but then the woman, still looking at me, slowly raised her hand and pointed over her head. I looked up. There it was, at least the corner of it, hanging over the edge of the one-story brick building: Wolcott Engineering.
>
>   Well, that's it, I thought. I tried. Monday morning the engineers would find a large mattress on their roof. It was out of my hands.

Not really. The story isn't just one guy anymore; I've created two other people, and they are in the mix, coming forward independently of the narrator's agenda. They are not going to slip away into the awful night so my guy can have his rueful thoughts, lonely and confused as he may be.

> §   The woman stepped up and tapped my elbow. "Back this around in the alley," she said. "Get as close to the building as you can."

When I read her lines now I am struck by how commanding they are, and naturally so. I realize as a writer lost in my story I was looking for all the help I could get, and when she offers these orders to the narrator it is simply following their agenda now. They want something and are going to participate in its getting.

§   "What?"

Again I'm going slow to find out. Remember this true thing: I am at the edge of the story, the way you are in a draft. Don't let the layout of this little essay trick you into thinking I might have known where this was all going from the outset. And so I've put myself in a position where the man can reiterate the terms:

§   "No problem," the man said. "We'll get your mattress for you; we got a deal going here, don't we?"

So now my next few steps are clear.

§   I backed into the alley beside Wolcott Engineering, so close I couldn't open my door and had to slide across to climb out. The woman was helping the man into the bed of the truck, and when I saw it was his intention to climb on the cab of the truck to reach the roof, I stopped him.

"I'll do it," I said.

"Then I'll catch it," he laughed.

The roof was littered with hundreds of green Thunderbird bottles glinting in the icy frost. They clattered under the mattress as I dragged it across to the alley. For a moment, it stood on the edge of the roof and then folded and fell, fainting like a starlet into the cold air.

By the time I climbed down, they had the mattress crammed into the pickup. It was too wide and

the depression in the middle formed a nest; the
man and the woman were lying in there on their
backs. "Two bottles," the man said.

"Don't you want to ride in front?"

"You kidding?"

What has happened by now because I've stayed through
this moment of unhappiness, confusion, and ambiguity is
that my two street characters have entered so fully into the
narrative that there has been a small but important trans-
action: I get to be them too. A writer wears every shirt.
Looking at the other stories I've published, I see in each a
moment (sometimes more than one) where I stand from
where I'm speaking for one character and go to the other
and strip down and climb into the new clothes. If a character's shoes are too tight, or too thin, or too heavy he car-
ries a different valence through the scene—every choice he
makes is adjusted. It's that old matter of *multiple remember-
ing*, of holding more than one agenda in your head at a time.
This is an elemental issue, I know, but I say truly that I write
it here again as advice for myself, for the next story. When
the man answers, "You kidding?" that is simply the reply I
would have given under these circumstances. Why would
anyone pass up the chance to ride in a mattress?

§   The Ford's windshield was iced, inside and out,
    and that complicated my search for a way out
    of the warehouse district. I crossed sixteen sets of
    railroad tracks, many twice, finally cutting north
    through an alley to end up under the Fourth South
    viaduct.

Again, I'm going slowly because I don't know the destination. I guess they're going to buy some whiskey as promised in the deal, but before they reach the liquor store, what more can I learn?

§   I heard a tap on the rear window. I rolled down my window.
"Could you please drive back across those tracks one more time?"
"What?"

What is right, since the narrator and the writer realize at the same time that they're hauling human beings in a mattress on a truck bed over rolling bumps in the night. It would be fun. The truth is (though as I write it is a distant memory) I've done it as a child.

§   "Please!"
So I made a slow circuit of our route again, rumbling over several series of railroad tracks: I'd adjusted the mirror and watched my passengers. As the truck would roll over the tracks, the two would bounce softly in the mattress, their arms folded tightly over their chests like corpses, the woman's face absolutely closed up in laughter. They were laughing their heads off. Returning to the viaduct, I stopped. The man tilted his chin up so he looked at me upside down and he mouthed: "Thanks."

They were laughing there; I believe it.
How much of a day's writing is about control? How much

is about letting go? There are clearly times when a writer keeps her head down, like Natty Bumppo on all fours looking for the tiny broken twig, the bent leaf, the footprint that will lead the right way. That posture is also really good for bumping one's head against the wall. There is a time to stand, look at the horizon, and try to find the pass between the distant mountains. My writing days are primarily the former activity. I follow the small clues closely, with some critical moments when I look up and try to find the true north of my plans. Most of my long-term decisions about a story (Will the barroom be big or small? Will the narrator be a nurse or a veterinarian? Will the two people be married?) are made away from the page. If I've decided that the story centers on two impoverished scholarship students in the Union Cafeteria or three blue-collar deer hunters camped out in the hills of Utah and then the material inventory that gathers around the group indicates that money is not an issue, then I'll follow that clue and adjust those elements of the material story, allowing it to evolve. Of course the room for the most evolution is early in stories when you know where the mountain passes are, but you're not sure of the company or equipment. In a draft I'll allow a character to change as the moment suggests, and I've had characters change occupations, stations, gender, and I've had them disappear outright or merge with another character. This makes for confusing spirals of first drafts, which is just fine; we can solve all the consistency issues later. The discovery process requires we listen *now*, that is while wading through the draft.

I'm deep into the draft of "The Governor's Ball" now, all big decisions feel like they've been made. I need to stay close, listen, watch. Fortunately I have one more station in my "plot"—the liquor store. On my way there, happily, luckily, I drive by this park, which is a real place of course, just a block from the liquor store. (Although that is irrelevant except to say that I'm not engaged in the vast magical acts of the "imaginative" process; I'm just typing here.) A writer can put the park and the liquor store anywhere she pleases. I mention the park here because there is an old locomotive in that park that—in a few minutes—will offer itself as a place for my story to close.

§   I cruised around Pioneer Park, a halo frozen around each streetlamp, and eased into the liquor-store parking lot.

"We'll wait here," the man told me. Inside, I was again reminded of how cold I was, and the clerk shook his head looking at my dirty clothing as I bought the two bottles of Old Grand Dad and a mini-bottle for myself. He clucked as I dropped the change. My jacket pocket had gotten ripped pushing the mattress across the roof; the coins went right through. My hands were cold and I had some difficulty retrieving the money. When I stood, I said simply to the clerk: "These bottles are all for me. I'm going to drink them tonight sleeping under the stars and wake up frozen to Third West. You've seen my kind before, haven't you?"

We know where that line came from. Its arrival is the benefit of staying in the room long enough to catch the echo of the dancer's remark. I know with certainty that if I'd stopped writing and gone fishing for two days and returned, this scene would have gone differently—without that echo.

§   Outside, I laid the bottles on top of my passengers, one each on their stomachs.

       "Many thanks," the man said to me. "It was worth it."

       "Where can I let you off?"

The answer comes to me as the only place I've already established.

§   "Down at the park, if it's no trouble."

       The woman lay smiling, a long-term smile. She turned her shiny eyes on me for a second and nodded. The two of them looked like kids lying there.

Now my story is over, in a sense. I have nothing more in the inventory. I know (whether I know it or not) that the narrator is not going to make it to the Governor's Ball. This is exactly a moment when a writer would look at the door, think about coffee, not without a feeling of satisfaction. I've typed ten pages or so, a paragraph at a time, what about a little break? What about giving it another twenty minutes? I'm going to stay right where I am; though I can sense again that the pace is going to change, slow.

§   I drove them back to the park, driving slowly around the perimeter, waiting for the man to tap when he wanted to get out. After I'd circled the park once, I stopped across from the Fuller Paint warehouse. The man looked at me upside down again and made a circular motion with his first finger, and then he held it up to signal: just once more.

I opened the mini-bottle and took a hot sip of bourbon. The park, like all the rest of the city, was three feet in sooty snow, and some funny configurations stood on the stacks of the old locomotive which was set on the corner. The branches of the huge trees were silver in the black sky, iced by the insistent mist. There were no cars at all, and so I sipped the whiskey and drove around the park four times, slowly. It was quarter to ten; Cody would have given my salmon to Dirk by now, saying something like, "He's been killed on an icy overpass, let's eat his fish and then dance."

I stopped this time opposite the huge locomotive. I stood out beside the bed of the truck. "Is this all right?"

The man sat up. "Sure, son; this is fine." They hadn't opened their new bottles. Then I saw that the woman was turned on her side. Something was going on.

Simply: this was a surprise to me.

§   "What's the matter? Is she all right?"

"It's all right," he said, and he helped her sit up. Her face glowed under all the tears; her chin vibrated with the sobbing, and the way her eyes closed now wanted to break my heart.

"What is it? What can I do?"

They climbed over the tailgate of the truck. The woman said something. The man said to me: "We're all right." He smiled.

"What did she say?" I asked him.

"She said thanks; she said, *It's so beautiful. It's so chilly and so beautiful.*"

That's it. A feeling struck me as I typed that last phrase, again spoken by the woman through the man, and the feeling was sharp and clear and best described as: *that's it.* The end. Yeah, but . . . part of me felt there were loose ends, loose something, but that was absolutely stilled by the last sentence. That's it; my draft is complete.

It is not my job to explain the story or understand the story or reduce it to a phrase or offer it as being a story about any specific person, place, or thing. My job is to have been true enough to the world of my story that I was able to present it as a forceful and convincing drama. Every story is a kind of puzzle. Many have obvious solutions, and some have no solution at all. We write to present questions, sometimes complicated questions, not to offer easy or not-so-easy answers. Do not be misled by the limited vocabulary the American marketplace uses to describe the possibilities for story and drama. If we're really writing we are exploring the unnamed emotional facets of the human heart. Not all emotions, not all states of mind have been named. Nor are all the names we have been given always accurate. The literary story is a story that deals with the complicated human heart with an honest tolerance for the ambiguity in which we live. No good guys, no bad guys, just guys: that is, people bearing up in the crucible of their days and certainly not always—if ever—capable of articulating their condition.

I wrote that word *beautiful* and stuck the period after it and knew my story was done. It was a bit of a surprise to me, and it took me a moment, but then I leaned back in my chair and the room came back for me and I got to blink and rub my face and see there on the desk where it had stood half full for over an hour, my coffee cup. There I was suddenly in my body again, unshaved and unshod and uncombed and unfit for company, and in that condition I stood away from my chair and left the room, stumbling downstairs to the un-made bed and the unvacuumed carpets and the unwashed dishes in the cold sink, and I was king of it all, master finally of my own house. I stood still and felt that end-of-story soli-tude that tells us all again the purpose of our houses, the windows, electricity, doors, running water. My heart swelled with pity for the drivers fleeing by and the days ahead when I would be among them, but for now I raised my arms. I had earned this house again, and I could jump around a little. Upstairs my first draft was complete, and now I still had forty minutes, which will always be more than enough time, to clean the house and shave and pour the wine.

The Governor's Ball

I DIDN'T KNOW UNTIL I HAD the ten-ton wet carpet on top of the hideous load of junk and I was soaked with the dank rust water that the Governor's Ball was that night. It was late afternoon and I had wrestled the carpet out of our basement, with all my strength and half my anger, to use it as a cover so none of the other wet wreckage that our burst pipes had ruined would blow out of the truck onto Twenty-first South as I drove to the dump. The wind had come up and my shirt front was stiffening as Cody pulled up the driveway in her Saab.

"You're a mess," she said. "Is the plumber through?"

"Done and gone. We can move back in tomorrow afternoon."

"We've got the ball in two hours."

"Okay."

"Could we not be late for once," Cody said. It was the first time I had stood still all day, and I felt how wet my feet were; I wanted to fight, but I couldn't come up with anything great. "I've got your clothes and everything. Come along."

"No problem," I said, grabbing the old rope off the cab floor.

"You're not going to take that to the dump now, are you?"

"Cody," I said, going over to her window, "I just loaded this. If I leave it on the truck tonight, one of the tires will go flat, and you'll have to help me unload this noxious residue tomorrow so I can change it. I've got to go. I'll hurry. You just be ready."

Her window was up by the time I finished and I watched her haul the sharp black car around and wheel into traffic. Since the pipes had frozen, we were staying with Dirk and Evan.

The old Ford was listing hard to the right rear, so I skipped back into the house for a last tour. Except for the sour water everywhere, it looked like I had everything. Then I saw the mattress. I had thrown the rancid king-size mattress behind the door when I had first started and now as I closed the front of the house, there it was. It was so large I had overlooked it. Our original wedding mattress. It took all the rest of my anger and some of tomorrow's strength to hoist it up the stairs and dance it out the back, where I levered it onto the hood of the truck by forcing my face, head, and shoulders into the ocher stain the shape of South America on one side. Then I dragged it back over the load, stepping awkwardly in the freezing carpet.

The rear tire was even lower now, so I hustled, my wet feet sloshing, and tied the whole mess down with the rope, lacing it through the little wire hoops I'd fashioned at each corner of the truck bed.

There was always lots of play in the steering of the Ford, but now, each time it rocked backward, I had no control at all. My fingers were numb and the truck was so back-heavy that I careened down Fifth South like a runaway wheelbarrow. The wind had really come up now, and I could feel it lifting at me as I crossed the intersections. It was cold in the cab, the frigid air crashing through the hole where the radio had been, but I wasn't stopping. I'd worried my way to the dump in this great truck a dozen times.

The Governor's Ball is two hundred dollars per couple, but we went every year as Dirk's guests. The event itself is held at the Hotel Utah, and the asparagus and salmon are never bad, but holding a dress ball in January is a sort of mistake, all that gray cleavage, everyone sick of the weather.

I was thinking about how Dirk always seated himself by Cody, how he made sure she was taken care of, how they danced the first dance, when the light at Third West turned green and I mounted the freeway. As soon as I could, I squeezed way right to get out of everybody's way, and because the wind here was fierce, sheering across at forty miles per hour, at least. The old truck was rocking like a dinghy; I was horsing the steering wheel hard, trying to stay in my lane, when I felt something go. There was a sharp snap and in the rearview mirror I saw the rope whip across the back. The mattress rose like a playing card and jumped up, into the wind. It sailed off the truck, waving over the rail, and was gone. I checked the rear, slowing. The mattress had flown out and over and off the ramp, five stories to the ground. I couldn't see a thing, except that rope, snapping, and the frozen carpet which wasn't going anywhere.

The traffic all around me slowed, cautioned by this vision. I tried to wave at them as if I knew what was going on and everything was going to be all right. At the Twenty-first South exit, I headed west, letting the rope snap freely, as if whipping the truck for more speed.

The dump, lying in the lea of the Kennecott tailings mound, was strangely warm. Throwing the debris onto the mountain of trash, I could smell certain sweet things rotting, and my feet warmed up a bit. By the time I swept out the truck, it was full dark. I still had half an hour to make the Governor's Ball.

I hit it hard driving away from the dump, just like everybody does, hoping to blow the microscopic cooties from their vehicles, but when I got back to Ninth West, I turned off. I didn't want to go retrieve the mattress; it was nine years old and had been in the basement three. But I had lost it. I had to call Cody.

The first neon I ran across was a place called The Oasis, a bar among all the small industries in that district. Inside, it was smotheringly warm and beery. I hadn't realized how cold my hands were until I tried for the dime in the pay phone. The jukebox was at full volume on Michael Jackson singing "Beat It!" so that when Cody answered, the first thing she said was: "Where are you?"

"I lost the mattress; I'm going to be late."

"What?"

"Go along with Dirk; I'll join you. Don't let anybody eat my salmon."

"Where are you?"

"The mattress blew out of the truck; I've got to go get it. And Cody,"

"What?"

"Behave."

It was not until I had hung up that I saw the dancer. They had built a little stage in the corner of the bar and a young girl wearing pasties and a pair of Dale Evans fringed pant-ies was dancing to the jukebox. Her breasts were round and high and didn't bounce very much, though they threw nice shadows when the girl turned under the light. I sat in my own sour steam at the end of the bar and ordered a beer. My fingernails ached as my hands warmed. All the men along the row sat with their backs to the bar to see the girl. I sat forward, feeling the grime melt in my clothes, and watched her in the mirror.

When the song ended, there was some applause, but only from two tables, and the lights on the stage went off. The barmaid was in front of me and I said *no, thanks,* and then she turned a little and said, "What would you like, Terry?"

I realized that the dancer was standing at my elbow. Now she was wearing a lacy fringed pajama top too, and I could see that she was young, there was a serious pimple above one of her eyebrows. I didn't know I was staring at her until she said: "Don't even *try* to buy me a drink." I started to put up my hands, meaning I was no harm, when she added: "I've seen your kind before. Why don't you go out and do some good?"

The barmaid looked at me as if I had started the whole thing, and before I could speak, she moved down to serve the other end.

It was a long walk to the truck, but I made it. January. The whole city had cabin fever. She'd seen my kind before. Not *me:* my *kind.*

The old truck was handling better now, and I conducted it back along Ninth West to Ninth South and started hunting. I'd never been under that on-ramp before, except for one night when Cody took me to The Barb Wire, a western bar where we watched all her young lawyer friends dance with the cowboys. In the dark, the warehouses made their own blank city. It was eight o'clock. Cody and Dirk were having cocktails in the Lafayette Suite. She'd be drinking vodka tonics with two limes. Dirk would be drinking scotch without any ice. He would have the Governor's elbow in his left palm right now, steering him around to Cody, "You remember Cody Westerman. Her husband is at the dump."

I crossed under the ramp at Fourth West and weaved under it to the corner of Fifth, where I did a broad, slow

U-turn across the railroad tracks to scan the area. Nothing. Two derelicts leaned against the back of a blue post-office van, drinking out of a paper sack. I cruised slowly up beside them.

"Hi, you guys," I said. It was the first time all day I felt fine about being so dirty. They looked at me frankly, easily, as if this meeting had been arranged. One, his shirt buttoned up under his skinny chin, seemed to be chewing on something. The-other had the full face of an Indian, and I was surprised to see she was a woman. They both wore short blue cloth Air Force jackets with the insignias missing.

"Have you seen a mattress?"

The woman said something and turned to the man.

"What did she say? Have you seen one?"

The man took a short pull on the bottle and continued chewing. "She said, *what kind of mattress is it?*' He passed the bottle to the woman and she smiled at me.

I thought: Okay. What kind of mattress is it. Okay, I can do this. "It was a king-size Sealy Posturepedic."

"King-size?"

"Yes: king-size. Have you seen it?"

He took the bottle back from the woman and nodded at me.

"You have? Where?"

"Would this king-size postropeeda fly out of the sky?" the man said. His eyes were bright; this was the best time he'd had all day.

"It would."

"What's it worth to you?" he said.

"Nothing, folks. I was throwing it away."

"You threw it all right!" the woman said, and they both laughed. I waited, one arm on the steering wheel, but then I saw the truth: these two were champion waiters; that's what they did for a living.

"Where's the mattress? Come on. Please. It's not worth anything." *There needs to be a pause here*

"Okay, what's it worth?"

"Two bottles of this," the man said, pulling a fifth of Old Grand Dad from the bag.

"That's an expensive mattress."

The man stopped chewing and said, "It's king-size." They both laughed again.

"Okay. It's a deal. Two bottles of bourbon. Where is it?"

For a minute, neither moved, and I thought we were in for another long inning of waiting, but then the woman, still looking at me, slowly raised her hand and pointed over her head. I looked up. There it was, at least the corner of it, hanging over the edge of the one-story brick building: Wolcott Engineering.

Well, that's it, I thought. I tried. Monday morning the engineers would find a large mattress on their roof. It was out of my hands.

The woman stepped up and tapped my elbow. "Back this around in the alley," she said. "Get as close to the building as you can."

"What?"

"No problem," the man said. "We'll get your mattress for you; we got a deal going here, don't we?"

I backed into the alley beside Wolcott Engineering, so close I couldn't open my door and had to slide across to climb out. The woman was helping the man into the bed of the truck, and when I saw it was his intention to climb on the cab of the truck to reach the roof, I stopped him.

"I'll do it," I said.

"Then I'll catch it," he laughed.

The roof was littered with hundreds of green Thunderbird bottles glinting in the icy frost. They clattered under the mattress as I dragged it across to the alley. For a moment, it stood on the edge of the roof and then folded and fell, fainting like a starlet into the cold air.

By the time I climbed down, they had the mattress crammed into the pickup. It was too wide and the depression in the middle formed a nest; the man and the woman were lying in there on their backs. "Two bottles," the man said.

"Don't you want to ride in front?"

"You kidding?"

The Ford's windshield was iced, inside and out, and that complicated my search for a way out of the warehouse district. I crossed sixteen sets of railroad tracks, many twice, finally cutting north through an alley to end up under the Fourth South viaduct. I heard a tap on the rear window. I rolled down my window.

"Could you please drive back across those tracks one more time?"

"What?"

"Please!"

So I made a slow circuit of our route again, rumbling over several series of railroad tracks: I'd adjusted the mirror and watched my passengers. As the truck would roll over the tracks, the two would bounce softly in the mattress, their arms folded tightly over their chests like corpses, the woman's face absolutely closed up in laughter. They were laughing their heads off. Returning to the viaduct, I stopped. The man tilted his chin up so he looked at me upside down and he mouthed: "Thanks."

I cruised around Pioneer Park, a halo frozen around each streetlamp, and eased into the liquor store parking lot.

"We'll wait here," the man told me.

Inside, I was again reminded of how cold I was, and the clerk shook his head looking at my dirty clothing as I bought the two bottles of Old Grand Dad and a mini-bottle for myself. He clucked as I dropped the change. My jacket pocket had gotten ripped pushing the mattress across the roof; the coins went right through. My hands were cold and I had some difficulty retrieving the money. When I stood, I said simply to the clerk: "These bottles are all for me. I'm going to drink them tonight sleeping under the stars and wake up frozen to Third West. You've seen my kind before, haven't you?"

Outside, I laid the bottles on top of my passengers, one each on their stomachs.

"Many thanks," the man said to me. "It was worth it."

"Where can I let you off?"

"Down at the park, if it's no trouble."

The woman lay smiling, a long-term smile. She turned her shiny eyes on me for a second and nodded. The two of them looked like kids lying there.

I drove them back to the park, driving slowly around the perimeter, waiting for the man to tap when he wanted to get out. After I'd circled the park once, I stopped across from the Fuller Paint warehouse. The man looked up at me upside down again and made a circular motion with his first finger, and then he held it up to signal: just once more.

I opened the mini-bottle and took a hot sip of bourbon. The park, like all the rest of the city was three feet in sooty snow, and some funny configurations stood on the stacks of the old locomotive which was set on the corner. The branches of the huge trees were silver in the black sky, iced by the insistent mist. There were no cars at all, and so I sipped the whiskey and drove around the park four times, slowly. It was quarter to ten; Cody would have given my salmon to Dirk by now, saying something like, "He's been killed on an icy overpass, let's eat his fish and then dance."

I stopped this time opposite the huge locomotive. I stood out beside the bed of the truck. "Is this all right?"

The man sat up. "Sure, son; this is fine." They hadn't opened their new bottles. Then I saw that the woman was turned on her side. Something was going on.

"What's the matter? Is she all right?"

"It's all right," he said, and he helped her sit up. Her face glowed under all the tears; her chin vibrated with the sobbing, and the way her eyes closed now wanted to break my heart.

"What is it? What can I do?"

They climbed over the tailgate of the truck. The woman said something. The man said to me: "We're all right." He smiled.

"What did she say?" I asked him.

"She said thanks; she said, *It's so beautiful. It's so chilly and so beautiful.*"

RON CARLSON was born in Utah in 1947; he attended the University of Utah where he received his BA and MA in English. He taught at the Hotchkiss School in Connecticut for ten years, spending his summers fishing and backpacking and writing in the West. He moved in 1981 and worked for the arts councils of Idaho, Alaska, and Utah. In 1986, he began his university teaching career at Arizona State University, where eventually he became Regents' Professor and Director of Creative Writing. He now teaches fiction writing at the University of California at Irvine.

Ron Carlson Writes a Story has been typeset in Minion Pro, a typeface designed by Robert Slimbach and issued by Adobe in 1989. Book design by Wendy Holdman. Composition at Prism Publishing Center. Manufactured by Versa Press on acid-free paper.